Praise for *High Performers*

Building success is a personal as well as professional challenge. Alistair Smith manages to get up close and personal in delving into the professional journeys of some successful schools.

He goes past the formulaic approaches, the templates for action and sets out a series of challenges for school leaders and their teams to ask themselves. The touchstone is a set of schools which are recognised as successful; most importantly by the pupils within them.

Because the book is not formulaic, it is one to dip into as a means of exploring your own school. Every section of the book bristles with the sort of reflection that touches nerves while at the same time offering balm.

The balm is the management suggestions that prompt a 'we could do that' outlook. The suggestions promote incisive, swift, modern and demanding but enjoyable approaches to leadership.

Alistair Smith leaves the reader professionally aware and personally motivated. Leadership can make a massive difference and young peoples' lives benefit when it does.

**Mick Waters, Professor of Education at Wolverhampton University,
President of the Curriculum Foundation**

I have never read a school improvement book like this. Almost every page has some small vivid, persuasive and compelling example of good practice drawn from the classroom or the department or the senior leadership team itself. Every one is authentic, as it would be with Alistair Smith as author. Generations of teachers and school leaders have known him as an inspirational speaker and workshop leader. Here he shows an enviable skill as a writer. It is written at a time when money is going to be tight but ideally every teacher should have their own copy. Even in such straightened times a copy for each newly qualified teacher and freshly appointed heads of department or subject leader would be money well spent by all schools. The beauty of this book is that it brings within your certain grasp what appeared just out of your professional reach.

Sir Tim Brighouse, Visiting Professor at the Institute of Education

Alistair Smith visited 20 of the top performing state schools to investigate 'what makes them successful?' He asked the same questions in each school and in *High Performers* he shares the findings. His style is lucid and pleasing; his findings reasoned and cogent.

I commend the book to school leaders and classroom practitioners. It gives persuasive evidence-based guidance on why some of the best have succeeded. It focuses on core purpose, student outcomes, learner engagement, classroom teaching, roles and responsibilities, professional development, managing data and the school as a community.

High Performers is an easily read and impressively practical 'how to' guide full of 'tips' that draw on original research.

Vanni Treves, Chairman of the Governing Council,
National College for School Leadership

I was once told that the more power you gave away the more power you had. If I had read this book earlier I would have understood the concept more fully. This easy-to-read book gets to the heart of distributed leadership. It creates a model which will help everyone within a school to understand its own unique core purpose and ensure that they feel empowered and accountable for delivering it. Whilst it will provide a brilliant 'big picture' guide for a new head it can be used as a service manual for experienced heads who are seeking to fine tune their leadership.

Will Ryan, Assistant Head of School Effectiveness for
Rotherham Borough Council, Education Consultant and Author

This excellent book, organised and written in a lively and engaging style, explains how schools can become high performing in all aspects of their work, based upon case studies, practice and extensive research. It is structured around the concepts of leaders improving, teachers performing and managers supporting with appropriate recommendations for action. The book is packed with practical ideas and suggestions and will appeal greatly to school leaders, classroom practitioners, members of the school community and all those who work and advise on school improvement.

Professor David Woods CBE, Chief Adviser for London Schools and
Principal National Challenge Adviser

Alistair Smith has set out to distil the practice of 20 high performing schools – and comes up trumps. The result is a highly readable book full of valuable practical advice. His lists of 'recommendations' for heads, teachers and middle leaders has the potential to inform, enliven and enrich many a discussion or training workshop. Reading this book is the first step for all those committed to school improvement – but I strongly suspect that it is the discussion that it provokes that will impact at both the individual and school level.

Sir Dexter Hutt, Chief Executive of Ninestiles Plus and Executive Leader, Hastings Federation

With characteristic wisdom and clarity, Alistair Smith peels back the layers of some of the country's top performing schools. What he reveals isn't some slick replicable formula, but there are some overpowering messages of what works – relentless sureness of purpose, the ability to say no, intolerance of mediocrity and endless optimism. Smith illuminates the schools he peers into with wit and humanity. This is no exercise in cheap praise or hagiography: he describes what he sees, what he's disappointed in or surprised by as well as what he admires. That's what makes the book such an illuminating, personable read. We look through the eyes of one of education's undoubted masters and find ourselves nourished and enriched by the account of what he sees. As a result, the seemingly impossible becomes tangibly more possible: without league table tricks or curricular sleights of hand, we could all make our schools like these. *High Performers* is a compelling read. It's strongly recommended for current and would-be school leaders, and also for our political masters who would benefit from this sharp-eyed, astringent and endlessly uplifting insight into what great schools do, day in, day out.

Geoff Barton, Headteacher, King Edward VI School

Every school leader will find a host of ideas in this gem of a book, which is packed with practical suggestions that are being used in outstandingly led schools.

The 93 recommendations – in separate sections for school leaders, middle managers and teachers – are a great resource for staff at all levels. Thoroughly researched and clearly presented, the book is an invaluable volume of excellent practice, which can be used in many different ways for professional development.

Every leadership team, middle management meeting and staff training day should focus on learning and this book will be a stimulus to improvement, whatever the starting point.

Every teacher and school leader will find in this book enough nuggets of wisdom to create a gold mine of good practice. The focus of the book is on great learning and it contains numerous examples of how it can be stimulated through great leadership and great teaching.

John Dunford, Chair of Whole Education and Chair of WorldWide Volunteering

The high performing school is an elusive phenomenon. We all know that it exists but actually identifying its component parts in a way that enables understanding and action is rare. This is what Alistair Smith has achieved in *High Performers*. This resource provides detailed and systematic guidance in how high performance actually works. Firmly based in current practice this book is both a reference work and a source of inspiration. It is challenging and practical and will be of real value to leadership teams planning their way forward.

John West-Burnham, Professor of Educational Leadership,
St Mary's University College

High Performers is a no nonsense, unapologetic plunge into what great success looks like. Using the brilliant metaphor of high wire performance Alistair Smith takes us into 15 extraordinary schools and shows us how leaders inspire, what high performing teachers do, and how middle managers support 'the human pyramid'. Every few pages, powerful, practical 'recommendations for leaders' are offered. An unusual and uplifting book.

Michael Fullan, Professor Emeritus, OISE/University of Toronto

Smith has a proven track record of success, established over a number of years, and his latest book should not be consigned to the bookshelf of unread self-help guides. On the contrary, this clear and accessible guide may help to inspire excellence in the places where it is needed most.

Trevor Averre-Beeson, TES Magazine

High Performers

Alistair Smith

The Secrets of Successful Schools

Crown House Publishing Ltd
www.crownhouse.co.uk
www.crownhousepublishing.com

First published by
Crown House Publishing Ltd
Crown Buildings, Bancyfelin, Carmarthen, Wales, SA33 5ND, UK
www.crownhouse.co.uk

and

Crown House Publishing Company LLC
6 Trowbridge Drive, Suite 5, Bethel, CT 06801, USA
www.crownhousepublishing.com

First published 2011. Reprinted 2011, 2012.

British Library of Cataloguing-in-Publication Data
A catalogue entry for this book is available
from the British Library.

10-digit ISBN 184590687-X
13-digit ISBN 978-184590687-0

LCCN 2010937327

Printed and bound in the UK by
Gomer Press, Llandysul, Ceredigion

Preface

The Flying Wallendas

The Flying Wallendas are a troupe of high wire performers. They first gained notoriety at a performance in Ohio in 1928 when the group fell from the wire. There was no safety net, it had been left behind in Germany, but they were unhurt. The next day, the newspaper report said: 'The Wallendas fell so gracefully that it seemed as if they were flying.' Karl Wallenda made his own name and that of the dynasty that day.

Over 80 years later his grandchildren, great-grandchildren, family, partners and friends still perform as the Flying Wallendas. The legendary Karl Wallenda died in March 1978 aged 73. Small and frail, halfway across a high wire suspended between two multistorey buildings and buffeted by winds, he sank on to, then fell off, the wire to his death on the streets of San Juan 300 feet below. A year later his grandson, Ric, completed the very same walk.

The Wallendas epitomise high performance at its best. They are wire walkers, human pyramid and trapeze artists performing without safety nets often in public spaces, across gorges and between skyscrapers.

Seen from afar the performers have a rhythm and style that looks effortless. Close up you would see the physical strain and sense the adrenalin. The Wallendas have legendary resilience, some would say an unhealthy indifference to risk. In 1962, whilst performing the 'seven-person chair pyramid' in front of a huge audience at the Detroit State Fair, the front man lost balance and three of the group fell – two were killed and one paralysed from the waist down. The following year the Wallendas took to the wire again. In one form or another they have been doing so ever since.

We are naturally curious about people who go out there and give their all; individuals and teams who bring something extra. This could be in the spectacle of the circus arena or stage or equally it could be in the pressured environment of a state secondary school like those described here. We are intrigued not only by the performance and the results but also the people behind the performance, the regimes they put themselves through, the routines they adopt and the beliefs that drive them.

Karl Wallenda was the inspiration of his troupe. His energy and vision drove the others on. His family and fellow performers adopted roles and were trained in different disciplines. Sometimes they performed solo or in a pair as trapeze artists, catchers or flyers. Sometimes as a team, perhaps the seven-person pyramid where everyone knew their job and did their job to work as a unit. Our high performers do more than entertain and enthral: they offer us a legacy, one that we can take to schools.

It's one of optimism about what's possible when we are prepared to take a few risks ...

Acknowledgements

Individuals, schools and organisations helped me in researching the content of this book and I am grateful for their assistance.

John Turner did a lot of the work behind the Outstanding and Beyond sections. Heather Hamer proofread sections of the book. David Douglass, Chris Montacute, Phil Bourne and Kirstie Andrew-Power at the Specialist Schools and Academies Trust helped set up the initial research.

The following head teachers also welcomed me to their schools and allowed me considerable freedom to ask questions of their staff.

Alan Gray: Sandringham School
Rajinder Sandhu: Guru Nanak Sikh Voluntary Aided Secondary School
Jonathan Miller: JFS School
Tracy Smith: Seven Kings High School
Doreen Cronin: St Richard's Catholic College
Rob Sykes: Thornden School
Iain Melvin: The Thomas Hardye School
Mark Johnson: St Angela's Ursuline School
Stephen Munday: Comberton Village College
Mike Griffiths: Northampton School for Boys
Caroline Hoddinott: Haybridge High School and Sixth Form
Jennifer Bexon-Smith: Tudor Grange School
Rachel Macfarlane: Walthamstow School for Girls
Nick Weller: Dixons City Academy
Jonathan Winch: Emmanuel College
John Winter: Weydon School
Chris Tomlinson: Chafford Hundred Campus
Ani Magill: St John the Baptist School
Ian Hulland: Alder Grange Community and Technology College
Oli Tomlinson: Paddington Academy

Mark Lovatt, Kenny Brechin, Darren Meade and Chris Harte from Cramlington Learning Village helped me with the new technologies referenced in the book.

Thanks to colleagues at Abraham Guest School, Wigan for their work on leader behaviours. Finally, to Ani for lots of support and encouragement and no small amount of inspiration.

Contents

Introduction:
The concept of high performers

This book explains how you can become a high performer and so help your school become even more successful – a high performing school, perhaps.

The book is the product of hundreds of hours spent in schools and it emerged from a research project completed with the Specialist Schools and Academies Trust (SSAT), which examined the leadership cultures in some of the most successful non-selective state schools in England. I visited 20 schools, 15 of which the SSAT had chosen as 'high performers' and 5 of which I added as my outliers.

The criteria for selection of the 15 core schools included:

- Outstanding in Ofsted (all categories)
- At least three years of progress
- Specialist Status from 2008 and prior to then
- Leading Edge Status
- CVA (Contextual Value Added) 2009 above expected
- Low internal variability
- JVA (Jessen Value Added) 5A–C 2009 equal to or above +10
- JVA 5A–C EM (English, Maths) 2009 equal to or above +10
- 2 A–C Sc (Sciences) 2009 above 54
- 2 A–C MFL (Modern Foreign Languages) 2009 above 32
- Non-selective.

The criteria for selection of the 5 'outlier' schools included:

- High or exceptionally high contextual value added
- At least three years of progress
- Recognised nationally for an aspect of their work in leadership or in learning

- Schools 'complementing' the core list by offering a novel dimension: for example, 'speedy' turnaround from category; innovation in parental engagement; outstanding succession planning; 'dramatic' intervention to improve results and imaginative work in learning

- Known to me.

Other schools cited in the book offered case studies of practice that I uncovered through reading, recommendations or conversations or from previous visits. The high performer model emerges from this work but also draws on the fact that over 20 years I have visited hundreds of schools, spoken to thousands of educators and delivered over 1,100 in-service events. Hang around long enough and something must rub off!

The schools that have been included do not claim to be the 'best' in the country, nor am I, on their behalf, making such claims. Some of the best leadership in the country takes place in schools where it goes unrecognised. Schools where, for instance, many students have everyday lives that are characterised by high uncertainty, dysfunctional relationships and poverty. For these students, their school is a reservoir of hope. There are schools that do terrific things in learning and teaching but are hampered by the absurdities of coping with endless bureaucracy, absurd regulations and an inspection regime which, all too often, misses the point and hands out 'limiting judgements' focused on peripherals. In years to come we will look back and ask ourselves how, as a profession, we allowed ourselves to label schools as failing with all the stigma, stress and consequence it carries because at the time of the visit the KS4 data hadn't been analysed by ethnicity.

Adjust the criteria for selection and you adjust the list of schools. It would have been possible to give a bigger emphasis to contextual value added, levels of progress from KS2 or the demographics of the catchment. The fact that every school acknowledged it struggled to create autonomous learners whilst at the same time improving their academic performance, suggests that for the schools here the definition of success needs to go beyond their exam pass rates.

In comparative terms the high performers sample is very small. There were 3,457 maintained secondary schools in England in 2003. There were 220 Leading Edge Schools from which the SSAT pick was made. The graphs below provide a sample of how our SSAT pick and outliers performed against Leading Edge Schools and all maintained schools.

KS2 to 4 progress in English and Maths 2009

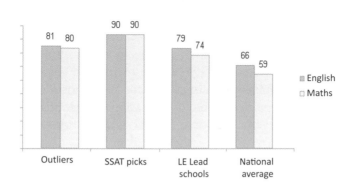

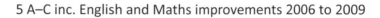

5 A–C inc. English and Maths improvements 2006 to 2009

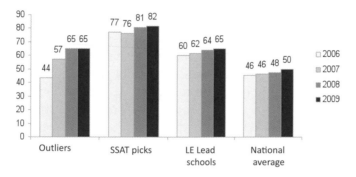

Jessen value added (KS2 to 4)
5 A–C inc. English and Maths 2009

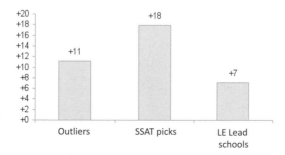

The 'research' has limitations. What was provided was a snapshot with visits confined to a limited time frame and schools choosing the staff interviewed. I was the only interviewer. There were limited opportunities for observation of classroom practice. The questions I asked were open to a variety of interpretations and inevitably respondents would wish to position themselves and their schools in a favourable light in answering them. There are hundreds of schools which do interesting and innovative work and do so in equally or even more challenging circumstances than those included here. However, to begin to account for every possible permutation in selecting high performers is a life's work. This is a snapshot of what some of the best have done to secure their success, no more than that.

In each of the 20 schools I visited I asked the same ten questions – in the same way – of three categories of educator: leadership teams, middle managers and classroom teachers. I was attempting to gauge what was the essence – or distinctive character – of successful schools, and what factors had shaped this essence. It was a study in school culture. I wanted to find out more about the everyday preoccupations and behaviours of influencers in successful schools.

Clear patterns emerged. Schools in the project were all well led. They had clarity around core purpose and said no to pressures or initiatives that threatened to divert them from core purpose. They were all stable with many, but not all, outward looking and eager to improve. All schools benefited from supportive parents though each had arrived at this positive situation by a different route. All schools were struggling to sustain high academic outcomes whilst at the same time creating more independent learners. Surprisingly for me, learning and teaching was not consistently good across these top-performing schools and, in fact, in some it appeared pedestrian. All schools managed student performance data effectively and most put it into the hands of teachers when they needed it most. Clear lines of accountability at all levels were apparent in nearly all of the schools, with the middle manager role seen as key. Staff development varied significantly – from practice that was in my view genuinely 'leading edge' to practice that had been the norm 30 years previously.

The high performer model assumes that leaders, managers and teachers all share responsibility for providing life changing experiences for the students in their care. In this regard they are like the performers in the main arena.

The leaders are high wire walkers who are visible to everyone, often – though not always – on their own, taking risks and showing a lead. This lead is based on years of experience, careful decision making and sensitivity to the changing environment in which they perform. The head teacher or principal is a high wire walker who stays focused on what matters, is relentlessly determined and looks ahead – not down or back. A word of caution for those who would walk the wire: becoming a head teacher is not the end of your journey. It's a higher and more conspicuous platform on which you must perform. Only go there if you are prepared for its particular demands and if you want to make a difference rather than have the role.

The teachers are the trapeze artists who know, understand and engage their audience with relentless optimism. Through great training and quality support systems, they are allowed to be and have become highly creative. They respect their performance medium and its inherent risks. They express themselves in ways that are often breathtaking in their individuality. They work tirelessly for perfection, they inspire – and never more so than in a choreographed small team performance.

The middle leaders are the human pyramid builders who work together building a solid platform that reaches up and up. They challenge expectation, provide support for others and show high levels of interdependence. Their success is based on strong bonds of mutual regard, trust and a capacity to micro-adjust, shifting weight and balance to keep the team aloft.

High performers work together and in doing so gain our admiration and respect. They do things we can mimic but never reproduce so the best we can hope for is to learn from them and create our own act.

One of the impulses to write this book was to let teachers, middle leaders and leadership teams see what the others needed to perform at their best. Most teachers don't buy books about leadership. Leadership teams have bought most of their teaching books, many of which now languish on the office shelves. Middle leaders don't seem to get many books written for them! So if I can do my bit to help each group widen its understanding of the everyday demands on the others then it can help elevate performance as a whole.

When I started the work on this book we were in the last days of a Labour administration. Now, as I finish, we are in the early months of a very different administration, a Conservative-Liberal one based upon a pact and one with a different set of emphases on education, assessment, inspection, learning and teaching. An hour ago the first White Paper was published. So for the performers, the wire has moved.

When the wire starts to move it's dangerous for the wire walker to try to stay still. The wire walker must adjust position and move with the wire. When the conditions change, adjust your stance but as you do so you must always look forward …

What's your school culture?

Culture in a school has been variously described as 'the way we do things around here' or 'the web of significance in which we are all enmeshed' or 'the shared beliefs and values which knit a community together'. In one study it's described as 'a reservoir of energy and wisdom to sustain motivation and co-operation, shape relationships and aspirations, and guide effective choices at every level of the school'.[1] One of the simplest ways to begin to understand the school culture is to undertake a learning walk.

A learning walk occurs when you, as a visitor, are accompanied around the school by a senior leader who tells you the story of the school as they see it. As part of my research I went on lots of learning walks. The 45-minute walk was deliberately chosen as my first exposure to the school. During the learning walk you can discover a huge amount about the school and how it seeks to position itself. Some of what you discover is anticipated, choreographed and deliberate. Most is unanticipated, unscheduled and arbitrary.

Schools are like individuals in that they seek to make sense of their everyday and present experiences by positioning themselves within a narrative. The school tells a story about itself and it is this story that unfolds as you are taken around the buildings and along the corridors. Your guide chooses to take you to places that are key to the story, often buildings of which they are proud or in some cases embarrassed; departments that achieve beyond expectation or facilities that are well used.

As you are taken around the school there is an accompanying story, which is often well rehearsed though never written down. The story can be positive and uplifting or it can be the opposite: either way it becomes the articulation of the culture of the school. I'd strongly recommend you avoid locking in your school to a negative or defeatist story.

Here are some negative or defeatist stories I've encountered in 20 years of visiting schools:

- we can't get good results because we are too near the airport and aspirations are low because of guaranteed jobs

- we are a seaside community with lots of seasonal workers

- we are a rural community and our boys just want to drive tractors and work on the farms

- we take our kids from that tower block

- we are too close to the industrial estate

- our corridors are so cramped the children misbehave

- our parents don't care

- we're on a split site

- the school opposite creams off the best youngsters

- we're only 20 minutes on the train to London

- the timetable won't allow it

- because of our geography we can't recruit good staff

- we've become the sink school for the town.

Allowing a negative story or 'script' to go unchallenged is to encourage it and give it a life of its own. Very soon it becomes the filter through which you make sense of things, to the extent that everyday behaviours, which in a wider context might seem eccentric, now are consistent with what the school has come to believe in and value, and so seem normal.

Recommendation for leaders: talk up the positive aspects of your school experience; do so relentlessly and unapologetically, and encourage others to do the same.

Before local events and circumstances begin to be 'your story' – intervene. Reframe what seems to be a difficulty into something more positive. The split site is an opportunity to have small schools within a larger school; the fact that you have one of the largest army camps in the country on your doorstep is also an opportunity to become the experts at dealing with behavioural issues to do with disrupted lives; if staff accommodation is prohibitively expensive form links with local housing associations; if you can't recruit because you are in an unattractive area have the best Continuous professional development (CPD) programme there is and promise young talent you will get them ready for their next move; if you tip into a category strip out every demand on teachers except that they prepare for and teach to the very best of their abilities.

Sometimes it is about small, gestural interventions. At Tudor Grange I was told that the term *non*-teaching staff was never used because the school did not have 'non' anything or anyone! When I interviewed Alan Gray, head teacher at Sandringham School, he never once used 'I', 'my' or 'mine'. I wrote it in my notes: 'he only ever talks about "we", "our" or "ours". At St John the Baptist School one of the first phrases to become popularised amongst staff was 'no winding down'. The head teacher had said it with

7

such regularity she began to be caricatured for doing so. At Chafford Hundred Campus the certificates belonging to all the catering staff are on display for all to see behind the serving area. Change their language, change your language, change what's seen and therefore change people's thinking.

Recommendation for leaders: use positive and inclusive words and images that have impact to communicate the best of your school.

A learning organisation is one that mines past and present experiences for important lessons and principles, for stories and legends that can energise current labours.

Deal and Peterson (2009)

There are only a few basic stories that humans tell. Some say only seven variations exist. Schools rework these basic stories much like authors and scriptwriters. Here they are with a school 'spin.'

1. Overcoming an adversary – we defeated the parsimonious local authority or the local predatory schools

2. The quest – we arrived together as a team and transformed the school

3. Journey and return – we had a transformational experience, which then influenced our thinking thereafter

4. Misunderstanding before resolution – the school had lost its way with too many directions and too many initiatives at once

5. Tragedy/hubris – the school was coasting and was hit by an inspection failure which it had not anticipated

6. Rebirth – we were a community school with a strong pastoral ethos; now we are an academy focused on attainment

7. Rags to riches – we were a failing school; now we are transformed.

Some of the stories are told in combination using a mix of three types of engagement: personalities, controversies or philosophies. I don't think this would matter at all if the stories told in those learning walks were one-offs. However they recirculate and obtain a life of their own. They are picked up by the community and by parents, they are invested in by staff, they may even go some way to framing the initial impressions of inspectors and perhaps play a part in judgements.

What really happens on a learning walk is that you are being positioned. This happens whether you like it or not. It may not be deliberate in any conscious or intended way but it leaves a trace. On the very first project visit I made in researching for this book, the deputy head took me on a walk around the school. It was a school of which he was genuinely proud. The walk was literally round the school and as we went around and outside we peered into classrooms, talked about the adjacent industrial estate and the football ground and the buildings. The deputy was hugely experienced, talking all the while with passion about the buildings and the people, the environment, stability, security and continuity. It turned out to be a very useful experience for me. The school's success was significantly influenced by the community it served and by stability, security and continuity. There were few risks taken in that school.

The research in study after study shows that when cultural norms were antagonistic to change, improvements did not take place. A group sense of efficacy generates energy towards improvement.[2] For head teachers and school leadership teams, when they talk about 'their' school they are talking about the things which are felt or agreed to be right and the things they feel or agree to be true. In other words, what you value and what you believe. The walk takes you straight to the heart of the school culture: what is valued and what is believed. For that reason I think it is a really useful exercise for a school to examine just what its culture may be and moreover what the signifiers of this culture are that are likely to be picked up and recirculated by stakeholders and others.[3]

Recommendation for leaders: **examine your school culture. Ask which cues a visitor might notice and, as a consequence, what conclusions they would reach.**

Summary of findings

Core purpose
High performers are very clear on core purpose and seeking consistency and coherence in its pursuit

Student outcomes
High performers strive to balance academic achievement with 21st century learning skills

Student learning
High performers actively engage students in being relentlessly optimistic about possibilities and their capacity to learn

Classroom learning
High performers progress from a performing orientation to a learning orientation

Curriculum offer
High performers relentlessly focus on what's best for *their* students

Professional development
High performers utilise both tacit and formal learning opportunities in perpetual support of functional and personal development

Staff roles, responsibilities and profile
High performers provide support, challenge and opportunity based on shared understanding of evidence

The school as a community
High performers celebrate successes and build a strong coherent team ethos with internal 'collaborative competition'

Engagement with parents and carers
High performers align with but are not dictated to by parental aspiration

Engagement with the wider community
High performers use partnerships to significantly extend their capacity to deliver an imaginative and enriching offer

Note: The 10 areas above formed the focus of the 10 x 10 Project upon which much of this book is based. Details of the 10 x 10 Project are also included in the appendices.

One:
The high wire – leaders inspiring

1. Core purpose
2. The first 10 steps
3. Academic *and* autonomous?
4. Staying the course
5. Saying no to peripherals
6. Exacting self-scrutiny

*Out on the wire is living,
everything else is just waiting.*

Karl Wallenda, high wire walker

Leader talk

The words and phrases most used by leaders in our interviews.

Staying focused

1. Core purpose

We keep really focused on core purpose.

Caroline Hoddinott, Head Teacher, Haybridge School

Start with this exercise. Get each person on the leadership team to individually write down what the school stands for; in other words, your core purpose. Do the same with governors. You may be shocked by how different the answers are! If you can't agree as a group of leaders what will the staff say? Many years ago I did a similar exercise with a school leadership team from a school in Somerset. I split the team in two and asked them to draw a representation of their school without any annotations or words. One group came up with a mountain complete with flag on top, different routes, fixed ladders and ropes, camps and guides. The message being whatever your starting point we can get you to the top. At the same time the other group drew a castle with ramparts, sentries, moat, drawbridge and portcullis. Their message was we need to be more selective about who we let in and once in, keep them under control. One school leadership team, but with two contradictory takes on core purpose.

Core purpose is not to be confused with school mission statements or ethos or values. By core purpose I mean those fundamental outcomes which are not for negotiation or compromise and which guide everyday decisions.

The 'core purpose' as defined by business writers Jim Collins and Jerry Porras, authors of *Built to Last*, is 'The organization's fundamental reasons for existence beyond just making money – a perpetual guiding star on the horizon: not to be confused with specific goals or business strategies.'

Core purpose ought to be capable of being boiled down to a sentence or two. One of the questions I asked of every interviewee – 95 individuals in total – was 'What is your school's core purpose?' In really successful schools there is always very strong coherence around core purpose. All staff are clear about what it is and what it isn't.

In times of difficulty core purpose will be put to the test. If you commit to provide *equality of opportunity for all* then it ought to shape policy and practice on permanent exclusions. If you declare yourself to *prepare students for the challenges of the 21st century*, why are you banning mobile phones? If you are a school that *values independent learning*, why are teachers marking every piece of written work?

Core purpose also guides the hard decisions about staff and staffing and could be valuable in determining the future direction of the school.

For example, a new academy had emerged from a previous incarnation as a community school and specialist college and was meeting as an extended leadership team to define priorities for the next three years. In years past its community provision – including extended hours, adult access, crèche and playgroup, evening classes and vocational provision – had been one of its characteristic successes. Now difficult decisions had to be made as to whether, in changed financial and demographic circumstances, it was possible to continue to serve the wider community.

Some of the most impressive schools had a core purpose, which was accurately and easily reflected in their school motto. Sandringham School in St Albans was 'Everybody can be Somebody'. Weydon School in Farnham was 'Inspiring Minds'. Chafford Hundred Campus had changed theirs from 'The School of the Future' to a more pragmatic 'The School for the Future'. At Walthamstow School for Girls the school motto 'Neglect not the gift in thee' is over 120 years old. In a full day session led by an external facilitator the whole school community revisited the school mantra, agreed to keep what was in place but modernised it to be more inclusive: 'Neglect not the gift in thee and nurture the gift in others'. This now allows the leadership team to test everyday decisions against the aspiration.

In the schools I visited I asked how student outcomes aligned to core purpose. The views expressed varied by status and experience. Senior leaders in all schools were clear on desirable student outcomes with most aligning to their core purpose. Middle leaders partly related it to the whole child and partly to academic outcomes. Junior staff were less clear and articulated it in relation to their own subject or in more vague terms like happy, fulfilled, good people or good citizens

Be quite clear that this is not about branding or about public relations. We know the corporate brands in part through their tag lines – *The Power of Dreams: Honda*; *Your Potential, Our Passion: Microsoft*; *Just Do It: Nike*; *Impossible is Nothing: Adidas* – but for schools it provides a benchmark for leadership to model everyday behaviours and decision making.

> *For us, Sewa – selfless service – is at the core of what we do.*
>
> Rajinder Sandhu, Head Teacher, Guru Nanak Sikh School

Core purpose also guides decisions about what is to be learned and how it will be learned especially when it ties directly into departmental planning and self-evaluation. At Chafford Hundred Campus – *The School for the Future* – each departmental plan must tie in to the four values of the school: learning, fusion, community and future. The detail of each is expressed like this:

- Learning – fostering a personalised, competence-led curriculum, which embraces broad choice within a vocational and enterprise oriented culture. Developing skills in both independent and collaborative learning to a high level.

- Fusion – engaging all groups from early years to adult learners in shared strategic planning, activity and evaluation; committed to the principles of an extended school with a fusion of phases and a lifelong learning agenda.

- Community – the campus at the heart and hub of this new, thriving and growing community as a centre for multi-agency activity in pursuit of excellence. Maximising the involvement of key stakeholders and other link organisations in shared strategic planning, activity and evaluation.

- Future – national and international 21st century school status, which is driven by excellence in the implementation of high quality effective e-learning, action-research models for staff development and a remodelled curriculum.

I think Chafford holds to the four values – learning, fusion, community and future – to direct everyday decisions and don't allow themselves to get lost in the semantics. All department plans, self-evaluation forms (SEF) and lesson plans are reviewed by the school leadership team each term. What's core is thus embedded into practice.

At Sandringham School in St Albans the head teacher and school leadership team use both the Year 7 and 8 assemblies and the Year 9 and 10 assemblies to influence the attitudes within the school. The phrase used to describe this was 'assemblies for cultural change' and the typical topics might be never giving up or on first impressions. The head teacher said that five years previously students were far less keen on receiving awards in public. Now celebration assemblies occur regularly.

At the JFS School in Wembley there is an aspiration that 'every student will become a leader' and this shapes a significant enrichment programme and what was described as a 'big debating culture'.

Revisit core purpose with all your staff and if necessary redefine it, check there is a shared understanding and put this understanding to the test. On a daily basis, abandon activities that do not serve your core purpose. As you work on core purpose try conducting a core purpose walk of your own.

Recommendation for leaders: be clear on your core purpose. It's not a catch-all mission statement. It's a definition of what's fundamental to your operation.

Spend 20 minutes walking around the school. Take a camera and start as a visitor to the school would by coming through the school gates on foot. As you arrive at reception look at the signage and the visual reference points particularly. Focus on this dimension and nothing else. Record the images you see: are they consistent with what you espouse?

What's it like to visit your school? What's the immediate visitor experience? In one school I visited in the summer of 2010, the first thing I was handed before signing in was a detailed checklist written by the school of nine things to do should a child approach me with a disclosure of sexual abuse. This was the first ever contact with the school. I was appalled. The message it gave to me, and the young people in the school, was treat *every* adult as a potential predator. Later I was told that the inspectorate had commented on this as outstanding practice. Whether this observation is true or not, I'm still appalled. In over 20 years of visiting schools this was the worst instance of misguided compliance I'd ever come across; just thinking about it now is getting me angry!

On another occasion I visited a school where, at the foot of a very large, prominently positioned, laminated 11-point mission statement, there were a further five points at the bottom of what the school did *not* accept – bullying and cruelty, cheating, lying and deceit, rudeness and offensive language. Really this is so misguided! A parent sitting opposite this would have their eyes drawn to this list and may not even notice the caveat above. As a general rule with visuals, which are public or student facing, they should reinforce learning behaviours that are desirable and are those you want; state them briefly, state them positively.

Top leaders are highly visible. They do not spend their days hidden in offices filling in forms. Only shut your door when you really have to. Be accessible and have your office in a busy area. Don't hide away. In a school we worked with, which experienced the amalgamation of two schools, the head teacher told me he obtained a really good deputy who was brilliant at detail, punctilious and good with data but not especially visible around the school. He arranged discreetly for the door of her office to be taken off its hinges. It's still off its hinges.

Your school leadership team needs to be comprised of good teachers who can deliver quality learning experiences in the classroom. They model and promote the behaviours that will drive core purpose. Together your leadership team will stop the school and staff doing good things to make time to do even better things. Each time you introduce something new, kick out something old to make the time for the new initiative. Use the school leadership team meetings for each member to say what they've done that week to earn their money and deliver core purpose. Get feedback from the staff. Ask them to say three things the school leadership team does well and three ways they could improve.

Remember saying no can be the hardest but is often most impactful part of leadership so get in the habit of saying no more often! You would be shocked to know of the sorts of things some schools took for granted that they had to do, that some of the top performing schools I visited would not even consider.

At Northampton School for Boys, Mike Griffiths, the head teacher, told me, 'We've turned non-compliance into an art form.' At Dixons Academy I was told, 'We don't jump on bandwagons, what we do is "Dixonise" the approaches which work for us. For example, assessment for learning is common sense not an initiative or an option so we develop it in our own Dixons way.'

At Walthamstow School for Girls the head teacher, Rachel Macfarlane, told me that the school had thought long and hard about being invited to federate with another local school but had eventually said no as it would not have been right for either school at that point in time.

At Thornden School, head teacher Rob Sykes said, 'There are huge swathes of initiatives we just refuse to do. You name a charter mark – we haven't got it!' He went on to add that they strictly limit the number of whole school objectives each year, typically it would be between four and six.

In some of the schools that were quick to articulate their independence from 'jumping on bandwagons' I could see when looking at their school development plans that the avowed position wasn't entirely borne out by what was revealed in their plans. There seemed to be a niggling need to cover one's back. It is very difficult to say no – especially so when the weight of a national or local authority initiative is pressing on you! With a change of government and a different expectation of what schools ought to deliver, some of the activities, which had been championed by the previous legislation and picked up in response by schools and written into their planning, have started to disappear. Where they no longer feature in discussion about whole school priorities one has to question their worth to the school in the first place. It takes considerable resolve to stick to the core purpose when others, including the inspectorate, may be asking you to evidence an alternative position. If it matters to you, your school and your students then it matters whatever the government, the incumbent secretary of state or the current orthodoxy.

The lesson from all of these schools is to be ruthlessly focused on core purpose so that staff are freed to do the same.

Recommendation for leaders: say no to initiatives and requests that do not serve your core purpose. Be ruthless in doing so.

2. The first 10 steps

The schools described here as high performing did not become so overnight. In most instances it was a journey of between five to seven years.[4] In the early months after taking over a new school as the head teacher, there seem to have been very obvious first steps on what had to be done.

At the Thomas Hardye School, Iain Melvin, 23 years a head teacher, described how 'In order to create a circle of virtue we had to initiate and live through a period of high control.'

Alan Gray, head teacher at Sandringham School, now describes his school as 'omnivorous' for learning but recognises that it has taken disciplined intervention to get there: 'Five years ago we got routines in place to skill people, good schemes of work made a difference, now we've gone beyond Ofsted.'

At Seven Kings School where student voice is very strong, work on assessment for learning had started with 80 students having a learning conversation with staff some eight years ago.

At Cramlington Learning Village my own 13-year association with the school allowed me to see their learning to learn journey, which began with the delivery of a discrete taught programme to one year group seven years ago. Now the school takes visitors from around the globe, keen to see what can be done with a whole school approach.

Recommendation for leaders: recognise that the journey to high performance may take five to seven years and plan accordingly.

Never waste a good crisis! Many head teachers used the term 'tipping point' to describe the single moment or the sequence of related events, from where the school felt like it had begun to lift. In some instances the head teacher and school leadership team deliberately engineered the moment. In others it came about through inspection. In others, it arose from a change of circumstance or an unforeseen event. The consistent feature is that the tipping point was followed by a release of energy. Some tipping points that were cited included:

- A positive inspection outcome – 'outstanding sets you free'

23

- A negative inspection outcome – 'we got a mandate for action, inaction was no sort of alternative'

- We broke through 80 per cent A–C – 'we'd never managed it in five years'

- Students became change agents – 'we decided to teach them the skills of learning'

- We appointed a data champion – 'being proactive on data gives you freedom'

- We lengthened the periods to 75 minutes – 'you can't wing it for 75 minutes!'

- Stirring up the hornet's nest – 'we did 300 fixed term exclusions in the first week, and then saw every parent, sometimes at 11 at night'

- Becoming a training school changed our ethos – 'we are big on improving others'

- Value added became the focus – 'we wanted to go beyond raw scores'

- Assessment for learning was introduced eight years ago – 'it's been a seamless progression ever since'

- Last year we had a push on passivity – 'our sixth form teaching was textbook led'

- Sponsoring an academy clarified our thinking – 'it made us revisit some of our basic systems'

- When we got the Ofsted call on the Friday I closed the school at 4 p.m. and it stayed closed over the weekend – 'I told the staff I trust you'

- Everybody got involved in reviewing the big policies – 'it brought us together'

- We suffered a very tragic bereavement – 'we suddenly discovered we were a uniquely cohesive community.'

Leadership teams exploit the opportunity to create a tipping point. All the head teachers of high performing schools I spoke to were acutely aware of the timeline to their current situation and the landmark points along the way. Here's a summary of the ten things that were consistently mentioned.

Step 1. Be visible and use the five Cs

From the first hours of day one the head teachers were seen by staff and students around the school. Visibility was cited as important for student discipline and for staff morale. At St Richard's Catholic College in Bexhill on Sea I was told by Glen Clark, the deputy head teacher, 'We are all out and about – in fact all staff do their bit – it's a 50-year-old building with tight corridors and cramped classrooms – the visibility of the leadership team is important in enhancing the respect culture.' Jules Durkin, a chemistry teacher for three years, said, 'Here I get to teach, there's less crowd control and it's all down to the school leadership team: they're always around, they're self-aware, they have high expectations and maybe it's also something to do with the Catholic ethos. Get out and about, stalk the corridors, go into every classroom. Be on the gates at the end of the day!'

Great leaders in any discipline and in any generation have a clear vision of what's to happen, they communicate it consistently and are resolute in its pursuit. For the head teachers I spoke to, the first two days of each school year, when all staff were assembled together, provided the seminal moment in communicating core purpose. One said she prepared this September input months in advance and worked hard to balance revisiting the 'school way' with additional and original material to keep staff aspirations high. Most head teachers talked about the crucial importance of speaking to staff about the way forward and using what was said as a mechanism for talking about and driving through change.

For these key presentations you will need the five Cs. Staff and the wider school community look firstly for the presenter, in this case you as the head teacher, to demonstrate Control. Is she in charge? Next they want Clarity. Is she sure of her ground? Next they want Coherence. Can I align my aspirations with hers? Next is Concern. Does she understand the challenges that I face? Finally there is Consistency. Will she also adopt the behaviours she espouses? The early sessions with the school community are opportunities to place energy, purpose and professionalism behind a shared core purpose.

Incidentally, when speaking in a public forum slow down! Most of us speak at about 120–125 words per minute. Research on Churchill, Kennedy, Mandela and Luther King showed they tended to speak at 110 words per minute. Martin Luther King's 'I have a dream' speech used only 88 words in the first minute. Pace is associated with presence (or lack of it).

In any school year there are fluctuations in energy levels. Don't try to change human behaviours when people are tired and at their most vulnerable. In schools, staff are vulnerable in the third week of November and in the third week of February and at points when energy levels are at their lowest. Humans have default behaviours that emerge in moments of stress. Expect to see some of these at these times. Other key moments when messages have to be spot on are the beginnings and endings of each term, the departure of Year 11 and Year 10 stepping up, staff in-service events and assemblies.

As a final visibility tip set a target for all members of your school leadership team to speak positively to each and every member of staff at least once every week!

Recommendation for leaders: **ensure the leadership team are visible and have a strong 'presence' around the school.**

Step 2. Take early action

In the schools I visited head teachers had secured quick wins and initiated slow fixes. The quick wins had often been small and frequently related to behaviour. It was not always deemed to be the substantive issue facing the incoming head teacher but action around it always had symbolic resonance. At Dixons Academy, Bradford, head teacher Nick Weller told me, 'The things you do are often symbolic: small things have great resonance.' Early on change something for the better!

For Alan Gray at Sandringham it had been his early and obvious commitment to address the issue of low-level persistent disruption in lessons with the senior leadership. Many teachers had found this to be very wearing so an intervention was welcomed by the whole community.

For Oli Tomlinson, principal at Paddington Academy, the quick win had been to be seen by the whole school community at the school gates at the end of each day eye-balling the gang leaders and dealers who threatened to wreck the lives of her students. For Alan Mitchell, the recently appointed head teacher at St Andrews School, it was the environment and appearance of the front of the school which needed freshening after years of neglect. These things are never done in isolation, there are always a hundred and one other things that are initiated simultaneously, but they are always picked up on and talked about. At Haybridge School some simple actions had symbolic value. For the then new head teacher, Caroline Hoddinott, one was removing the bells to indicate changes of lesson. It represented a change of approach and a shift in relationships towards something more mutual.

As a head teacher you may want to consider the value of abandonment. Some of the best quick wins involving replacing the to-do list with a no-longer-do list. Go to the staff and ask, 'What sorts of everyday things can we readily abandon without compromising on our core purpose?' Give them a week to think about it and email you a well considered personal list.

Once a year ask one of your administrative team to help you itemise all the requests sent to staff that required some sort of written response. Take the completed list and then annotate each according to time required to respond and impact on the life of the school. For time: A is less than ten minutes; B is ten minutes to an hour; C is over an hour. For impact: 1 is significant impact; 2 is partial impact; 3 is limited or no impact. Plot these on a graph and stop doing 3s and C2s straight away and review the rest.

Generally speaking a quick win can be initiated by a unilateral change of policy, rule or routine. Slow fixes usually involve changing behaviour and that always takes time. Of all the time demanding slow fixes, changing the behaviours of teachers in the classroom is probably the most difficult but certainly the most significant.

Recommendation for leaders: **obtain quick wins and initiate important slow fixes.**

Step 3. Get the basics in place

At any given moment there is a high probability that a low probability event will occur – so be ready for such moments! However too many of these moments is a sure fire guarantee that you do not have the basics in place.

There are minimum standards to everyday conduct acceptable within a school community. To drop below this standard is to flirt with a dangerous and downward spiral. In every school I visited there were countless incidents of staff correcting small misdemeanours, picking up litter, adjusting ties, tucking in shirts. There was never an instance of a school community attributing responsibility for the micro-management of the everyday conduct and behaviour of students to senior staff. In successful schools there are always lots of teaching staff on duty. They can be seen interacting positively with the students, building little informal pockets of knowledge to give their relationships an additional dimension.

Walk the school three or four times a week. Ensure that a member of your school leadership team is designated each day to look in on lessons every period. As one head teacher put it to me, 'Walking the school is good for your soul.'

In an Ofsted case study cited about Robert Clack School in *Twelve Outstanding Secondary Schools: Excelling Against the Odds* it describes how the head teacher began touring classrooms and using assemblies to tell students how he wanted them to behave. He also used what he termed the 'mystery power' of the governing body to endorse any 'hard line' he felt he had to take: 'The governing body is giving me clear instructions there is no slippage on behaviour.'

The school leadership team at Sandringham said that 'After fire-fighting for 18 months we finally embedded and systematised the rewards and consequences and it meant an end to low level disruption.' Ensure your behaviour policy is regularly updated, is simple, understood by everyone and displayed everywhere in language as positive as you can make it.

Go for something that is paper free. Move away from a behaviour strategy generated by a policy written some time before in an 'ideal' environment which requires a member of staff to fill out an incident form, copy the form, submit the form and then wait, wait, wait. Dealing with behaviour issues, especially with staff and leadership teams who are young and inexperienced, needs to be driven by what works in practice not by what works in policy.

In 100 per cent of cases bad behaviour needs to be dealt with there and then. Dissent and defiance double with delay. The idea of a weekly or fortnightly detention, which sucks up all the miscreants and puts them in a room to be supervised by a member of the school leadership team, is ruinous. Abandon it in favour of an approach that favours and gives authority to your teachers at the point of need. Misguided approaches to discipline are the number one cause of staff stress and resentment. Persisting with the unworkable will lead to lower morale and staff absence. Once teachers have the authority and the capacity for immediate action be explicit in helping them understand that behaviour in their lessons is now their responsibility. They must exercise their authority and sanction children themselves before passing it on. If there is poor behaviour in most of their lessons, their teaching and general classroom management may well be at fault.

Recommendation for leaders: secure a framework for discipline and standards, and strive for consistency of response to incidents from all staff.

Step 4. Make learning more engaging

What happens to students in your classrooms should drive your thinking. Is the quality of their experience good enough? If not what are you doing about it?

For head teacher Rob Sykes, it's important to have highly engaging lessons: 'Our top students can be badly behaved if the teacher or the teaching isn't good enough and it's not about giving them knowledge, it's about working alongside them. Rob describes how he and his team at Thornden had been heavily 'interventionist' at first, putting lots of time into getting quality schemes of work and lesson plans across the school and introducing guidelines for teaching and learning to be 'applied as much as possible in every lesson'. The guidelines, which are reviewed annually, cover planning and starts, behaviour management, expectations and assessment, homework and endings. Rob went on to add, 'I see a danger in leadership teams doing too much of the wrong work, accentuated by Ofsted; there can be too much monitoring and not enough support. Also there comes a point where once you have got the basics in place the teachers need the freedom to fly if they are to aspire to the highest standards.

A simple yet powerful tool is to begin to design learning experiences by drawing from an inventory of agreed features and against a learning model such as a cycle or sequence. There are two aspects to this. The first is to build understanding of what is known about the science of learning and the principles that underpin it. The second is to deploy those same principles using a variety of techniques. Being able to do so in different contexts is the art emerging from the science.

At Chafford Hundred Campus their 'What does great learning look like?' checklist guides and is included within every lesson plan, forms the basis of lesson observations and learning walks with every lesson plan audited by the school leadership team once termly. It drives the accountability cycle, which is one of the outstanding features of the school.

Don't wait for behaviour to be sorted or for behaviour policies to kick before working on improving learning. Students are all entitled to engaging, relevant and challenging learning experiences. Inevitably a few will kick up if any of these variables are missing. Aim to factor out poor teaching and inadequate learning as a contributory cause of misbehaviour.

International research cites the quality of what happens in the classroom as the key driver for school success. Again and again we see research from all over the world telling us that an effective school is full of effective classrooms.

Recommendation for leaders: **insist on lessons which engage, have pace, structure and challenge. An effective school is full of effective classrooms.**

Step 5. Review the curriculum offer

A and O level qualifications were introduced in 1951. The world our children will inherit has changed out of recognition in the last half century yet we test in the same old way. We know more about learning, the human brain, motivation and applications of technology than ever before but the A level remains the gold standard. Questions have to be asked!

Start by asking some of your own about your curriculum offer. Here is a sample:

- What's the value to the end user? How does what you offer advantage them in life? Are you doing more than transiting them efficiently to the next stage? Is there any point in force-feeding them through sixth form so they can drop out in the first year of higher education?

- How much effort do you put into getting students to elect suitable subjects for Year 10 or for the sixth form? Does everyone have an individual interview? How frequently would you say no? Is it analysed?

- Does the duration of lessons in your school, your learning day and week, support your aspirations for learning? Short periods can hide weaker teaching and are not necessarily best for learning. Should you be lengthening yours? Do all lessons need to be the same length?

- Is the breadth of what you offer right? Too much is as bad as too little. Too much extends your resource and your flexibility of response. How many GCSEs do your students take? Do all take the same number? If so why?

- Can you track your offer by having gold, silver and bronze with different provision for each track?

- Do you offer sufficient quality provision for weaker students? For example, ASDAN CoPE or OCR science.

- If your students have poor English language skills what more can you do about it?

- How useful is early entry? Half of our project schools are backing off from it. Why do you do it?

- What's the balance between academic provision and vocational? Within your academic provision, what percentage of student commitment is taken up by following the 20 subjects deemed by Cambridge University to be second or third division?

- Are there enough options for weaker to average students in your sixth form? For example, Salters' Chemistry, the University Award, travel and tourism, health and social care, BTEC sports, public services, photography.

- Is your vocational provision in place in order to get 'bums on seats'? What's the fallout from a bums on seats approach?

- How do links with other providers add depth to your offer? For example, universities, local businesses, professional sports clubs.

- Can you add a sixth period to offer things students would really like to do such as whacky science, horrible history, online gaming and dangerous sports?

A good curriculum, which is well taught and accessible, will remove lots of behaviour problems. Many behaviour issues arise when students have such low literacy skills they are unable to access what's on offer. Intervention programmes such as Reading Recovery and resources such as Accelerated Reader are used to remediate the situation as quickly as possible in Year 7. Think outside the box on this: at Chafford, media studies has been really helpful using different sorts of texts to engage boys. At St Bonaventure's in Forest Green, changing the title of extra English as an additional language (EAL) Saturday sessions to 'improve your academic English' (IAE) resulted in a 100 per cent attendance improvement.

Anthony Seldon, principal of Wellington College, claims that 'few state schools offer the same opportunities for holistic education as independent schools'.[5] Adding that they should 'provide opportunities for developing each child's personal qualities, as does the International Baccalaureate's (IB) "learner profile" and in the IB's "areas of interaction"'. Coverage can be the enemy of learning. The more we cram the curriculum with content and use precious time for the assessment of knowledge of that content, the less space we leave for individual growth. He may have a point.

Think about alternative provision that is genuinely alternative. If you sincerely aspire to be 'world class' in learning then you are not going to become so offering GCSE and A levels in timetabled slots. I'm sorry but no one is getting on a plane from Sydney, Seattle or Szechuan to travel across the world to see how you do this!

Recommendation for leaders: ask hard questions about what's on offer in the curriculum and how it is accessed.

Step 6. Build the school as a community

On day one ask all your staff – including support staff and site management staff – to think about then write down:

- three things that are done well and we must keep or build upon
- two issues that must be addressed immediately
- one piece of advice you would give to the head teacher and the school leadership team.

Small things make a big difference so work hard to create a reciprocal culture. This means you work hard to make it easier for teachers to teach and for others to support their teaching. The job of the leadership team is to support the staff, not catch them out, so 'praise in public and pressure in private'. Don't sweat the small stuff. If a member of staff wants to go to an event which has personal significance such as a wedding or graduation, make it possible. Let them go and pay them – you'll get paid back in triplicate.

Make sure you have an appreciation strategy. Who gets thanked and for what? Also who gets invited to the celebrations and parties – extend the invite to the wider school community as far as possible.

At Haybridge School, head teacher Caroline Hoddinott gave everyone in the wider school community – teachers, support staff, site maintenance staff, caterers – a £50 voucher to spend on improving the school from the school developmnt plan (SDP). In one step it was a brilliant way of building affinity for, and a sense of pride in, the school and its environment. People could spend it on anything they liked. For example, six of the cleaning staff pooled their vouchers to buy a water feature for an open area of the school, designated as a peace garden; lunchtime supervisors bought goalposts: I'm told they patrol and guard them jealously. In another school each term every member of staff is given another member of staff to 'adopt'. Over the course of the term they must do three things to make that person's life easier – however each intervention must remain entirely anonymous!

One of the small things that has great impact is the video recording of student reactions as they get exam results in August. This took place in six of the schools I visited. At Seven Kings a camera team of ex-students is used to film and interview students. Excerpts are cut to uplifting music. The video is shown to staff on the first day back. The head teacher, Tracy Smith, told me that a member of staff watched it when she was feeling tired and questioning herself and it immediately rejuvenated her. Spread the positivity around! For new staff make sure one of the school leadership team sees them at the end of every day to ensure they are settling in and don't need any additional help.

At Seven Kings the imaginative design and build of a restaurant within a very confined space was more than an attempt to improve standards of cuisine; it was also a deliberate intervention to raise the number of opportunities students had to practise social skills and mix with others. At Walthamstow the tables in the restaurant are deliberately round and small to encourage group interaction.

At Sandringham the staffroom contains a 'learning wall' with the learning and teaching focus for the year and recommended strategies. The school improvement plan is displayed as a large three-dimensional display of the seven building blocks of the school. It's an effective way of communicating school priorities to all staff and was used to help with newly qualified teacher induction. Students are sometimes invited to the staffroom for the briefing and particularly the learning tips section to give their opinion on the tips and which they think work best.

At Tudor Grange, sponsoring an academy clarified their thinking and as part of an attempt to change the culture it was felt that they needed to revisit fundamentals such as levels of service. Having redesignated the canteen the 'restaurant', provided smaller tables and modernised the look of the place, time was spent with catering staff on things like meeting and greeting, dealing with difficult student behaviour and being positive about their contribution to the life of the school.

If you have a house system make sure all staff belong to one of the houses. Include catering staff, site maintenance staff, technicians, mentors and governors. Have them wear badges to increase the community feel.

Have a 24-hour guarantee turnaround period if staff request support. Ensure you close the loop within the 24 hours. If staff criticise the school leadership team it is usually for lack of support when they ask for it. Never make staff sign compliance agreements, pay for tea and coffee or conform to trivia designed to save a few pounds here and there. It backfires and no one works productively in a coercive environment. In one school, where heads of year were asked to sign compliance agreements, one subsequently claimed half a mile travel, not because he wanted the money but because he resented the system: treat people with contempt and expect a backlash.

Recommendation for leaders: **build a sense of community through shared successes, symbolic moments and interventions.**

Step 7. Provide challenge and support

Within the first week some head teachers will have assessed the staff to identify any gaps. Three things then follow. The head teacher will have begun to formalise a view on green light teachers – who are good and need encouragement and support; amber light teachers – who are not so good but want to be and may be capable of becoming better with support; red light teachers – who are not good enough and either don't want to become better or are not capable of becoming better and so must move on. Too often, mediocre schools tolerate mediocrity in their classrooms. This is the elephant in the room. Most teachers do a heroic job in challenging circumstances but for a tiny few the light has gone out or was never there in the first place and at some point someone has to say so.

Energy is put into recruiting, borrowing or seconding quality teachers to fill vacancies. Senior leaders who may not be teaching but who are good teachers are put with 'at risk' groups especially exam groups in Year 11, and heads of department are asked to ensure that the best teachers are not 'hogging' the top sets.

Kenneth Leithwood's work[6] on transformational leadership suggests that teachers' motivation for development goes up when *leaders give staff a role in solving non-routine school improvement problems.* According to Leithwood, 'Transformational leaders involve staff in collaborative goal setting, reduce teacher isolation, use bureaucratic mechanisms to support cultural changes, share leadership with others by delegating power, and actively communicate the school's norms and beliefs.'

Introduce simple-to-follow quality standards in the form of guarantees. For example, at St Richard's there is an expectation of a two-week turnaround on all marking. Parents who phone the school are entitled to and can expect to receive a return call within 24 hours.

Find ways to involve the staff in the future direction of the school without creating extra work for them. For example, have a staff meeting about the school development plan and get staff to sign up to one section they are interested in and just brainstorm ideas of how the school could move forward in that area. Everyone has the chance to input and exercise choice.

Make sure that your CPD provision is second to none. Balance tacit – on-the-job – learning with formal learning. Make sure you have strong, differentiated in-house support programmes with a big emphasis on classroom practice. Challenge your staff to be the best professionals they can possibly be. This requires constant reflection upon, and improvement of, their classroom practice.

Recommendation for leaders: let staff know that if they do their best for students you will support them provided their best is good enough and if not, you will act.

Step 8. Get on top of the data

You need really good data – we are pretty clear on incontrovertible data. Being secure and proactive on data gives you freedom. All staff must be familiar with the data and if students aren't making the progress in line with or exceeding the data then we have the conversation.

Stephen Munday, Head Teacher, Comberton

Have a very clear strategy for obtaining pupil performance evidence, interpreting it and putting it into the hands of those who need it most at the time when they need it most. Each of the schools I visited was right on top of data. This was fundamental to their success. There were no surprises on results day in August. No subject heads sitting with the school leadership team in September at a loss as to how to explain what's happened.

As the head teacher, do you know which of your students is on free school meals? In 2009 out of an original cohort of 600,000 students across England there were 80,000 children on free school meals. Of this group of children, a total of 45 got into Oxford or Cambridge University. This total is less than the number from Eton College, Harrow or St Paul's Schools. Statistics like this should make us all feel uneasy.[7] If you do feel uneasy about this statistic then the presentation of the data is having its desired effect. Without the hard evidence, without data, it's just opinion. Make the hard evidence available.

Work out the value added for every student, every class and every teacher within the subject and publish it to the staff. Focus on the positive and share best practice on how to raise achievement. Be brave. Staff will get used to it.

At Thornden School, every teacher gets data on a single sheet on every child they teach who may be at danger of under-performing at KS4. Targets are 'bottom up' based on what Thornden pupils have achieved in previous years rather than 'top down' based on national data. The data each teacher gets includes the student's name, picture, CAT score, predicted grades and a short summary of behavioural issues or any special needs. The data is used by teachers to help with class seating plans, pairing or 'buddying' pupils, coursework, homework, choices of exam papers and for differentiating activities. Groups such as high achieving but 'lazy' boys, students on borderlines such as C/D or those at risk are flagged up by the head of year and a range of strategies can then be triggered: paired with a mentor, focused attention, extension or revision lessons, home liaison.

Walthamstow School for Girls is another example of a school on top of the data. September analysis of the GCSE results looks at raw outcomes, value added and the residuals KS2–3 and KS3–4. All teachers get a copy of their results, work out their own value added and then add their own contextualising comments. All data is instantly accessible on Resource Manager and it is managed by a dedicated specialist. The information that flows out to staff includes class lists with details of KS2 levels, special educational needs, free school meals and gifted and talented. Seating plans are based on this data and revised termly. Faculty meetings review individual students' progress. If any look in danger of underperforming by two levels or more from the upper quartile it triggers in-school support and an explanatory letter home. The whole premise is one of 'intelligent accountability'.

Recommendation for leaders: **get on top of the data, tighten monitoring and accountability and be open and honest to take staff with you.**

Step 9. Build productive partnerships

There are many valuable opportunities in partnering with others. This will be increasingly necessary in times of shrinking support networks. One really vital partnership is with Initial Teacher Training (ITT) providers or with those partners with whom you can provide ITT.

At the Thomas Hardye School, the head teacher, Iain Melvin, told me that their involvement with the Dorchester Area Schools Partnership (DASP) and Plymouth University allowed them to run their own accredited leadership programme and their own newly qualified teachers (NQT) scheme, and when they appointed newly qualified teachers it was not because they were cheap but so they could 'mould them with high octane expectation'.

In the Ofsted publication *Twelve Outstanding Secondary Schools: Excelling Against the Odds*, the case study of Challney High School for Boys describes how a School-Centred Initial Teacher Training (SCITT) programme was soon set up and, working with other schools across Luton, a training centre was established to train staff for all schools in the area. Chiltern Training Group Luton has now trained 50 per cent of its own staff and 15 per cent of the total teaching force in Luton with a high representation from the local community. The spin-offs are reported as being impressive with over a thousand teachers and support staff trained.

Ensure your governors are ambassadors for the school within the local community and with strategic partners. Ask individual governors to assume responsibility to build partnerships with targeted groups or sectors from your community and beyond: arts organisations, sports clubs, businesses, community groups, local media. Don't try to do it yourself.

The times they are a-changing – whilst this book was being researched all of the schools had benefited from targeted funding. This included money from a first and in some cases second or third specialism, Leading Edge funding, Gaining Ground funding, Gatsby monies in some schools and funding streams related to other initiatives helped with staffing, training in and outside the school and partnerships with other schools. Some of this funding will go and therefore threaten some of the partnership activities. It's never been more important to dispense with unproductive relationships and build partnerships that will help your school deliver its core purpose.

Recommendation for leaders: start to build productive partnerships but focus down to the 20 per cent which will give you the 80 per cent return.

Step 10. Make it safe for learning to occur

The street stops at the gate. Don't countenance street values in your school. Go to the front gates and draw a white line across the point where school values begin. Use the line as a metaphor to help students, particularly more troubled students, transit to responsible learning behaviours when they are within the school. Make the point whenever you can, in whatever way you can, that the school is and always will be a safe haven for learning.

Get your teachers to spend half an hour with the child they find most difficult. They should use this time to get to know them and what makes them tick. This will have dramatic effects.

At Chafford Hundred Campus the head teacher, Chris Tomlinson, commented that his parents and families were from Essex, many originally from the East End of London, and they were both clear about what they wanted and didn't want and also very vocal about it. They, he said, wanted immediate access to him; they wanted to see him around the school and on the gates; they were often critical and he needed big shoulders. Their demands had influenced the curriculum offer, which is both highly personalised – KS4 starts in Year 9 with over 50 option choices – and provides high perceived value. In his words, 'We don't do anything other than solid, recognised qualifications. Our parents don't want two for the price of one or cornflake packets; they want what the kids in the independent schools get ...'

A number of the schools I visited actively sought to preserve the small school feeling within the larger school. Cramlington High School redesignated itself Cramlington Learning Village in 2009 and deliberately set up three small schools or 'villages' within the larger school community. This was in an attempt to create more local autonomy for leaders but also to allow students to feel part of a smaller community where they would be recognised and valued. At Haybridge, KS3 has moved to two years and KS4 to three; Year 7 pupils spend a lot of time learning how to learn, be proactive and problem solvers. The sense of a smaller, more intimate community helps.

Recommendation for leaders: **build a safe environment with strong school values where students and staff can focus on and enjoy learning.**

3. Academic *and* autonomous?

We asked parents, students and governors if they could make one change what would it be – they said, learner independence.

Tracy Smith, Head Teacher, Seven Kings School

Creating autonomous learners who are self-managing, skilled in the techniques of learning and enquiry and who, at the same time, will also achieve the best possible exam results is the issue facing all of the schools.

In the visits I made to 20 schools, 15 of which were SSAT picks, I found an interesting pattern. All 15 and each of my 5 outliers, that is a total of 20 schools, were wrestling with the problem of creating independent learners whilst at the same time delivering ever improving academic results. Many talked of force-feeding at KS4 and then paying the price for having done so at KS5.

Jonathan Winch, principal at Emmanuel College said, 'We have a huge challenge to overcome spoon-feeding.'

Jonathan Miller, head teacher of the JFS School said, 'We are on a journey – we need to revisit what makes good learning.'

At Tudor Grange, Solihull, Jennifer Bexon-Smith observed, 'We had been a conveyor belt – now there is a fight here between teacher input and learner independence.'

At Haybridge the school joined the Innovation Unit's Learning Futures project in order to 'tackle the perceived disparity between the prescriptive tendencies of mainstream school pedagogy, and the creative and independent thinking skills demanded by undergraduate study'.

Sandringham School has a two-year project focusing on independent learning, particularly at KS4, the platform for which are the independent learning action plans created by each faculty. In faculty schemes of learning there is a specific requirement to integrate independent enquiry, one of the Personal Learning and Thinking Skills (PLTS).

At Thornden, head teacher Rob Sykes said, 'Schools have to work with the examination and assessment structures they are given. If employers and society want independent learners then those structures need to be changed.'

All of these high performing schools are aware of the issue but what they are doing about it tells us a great deal about the differences between them. Of the 20 schools I would say that one group were forward thinking and outward looking in their approach to learning; another were transiting from more traditional and teacher-led methods towards a more flexible repertoire; and another group, perhaps three, possibly four schools, whilst aware of the challenge did not appear to be engaged with issues of learning and teaching in a coherent *whole school* way at all.

Other schools who are seeking to or being pressured to, select students can become more performance and outcome oriented. This can inhibit a learning orientation, with opportunities to develop and practise the habits of independent learning declining as students move towards their public exam years.

Recommendation for leaders: confront the challenge of creating autonomous learners who are skilled at learning and are also academically successful.

In the 2007 NCSL publication *What We Know About School Leadership* (2007a), it states in the summary of key points that learning-centred leadership is critical in schools and breaks this aspect of leadership down into six components:

- lead by example
- monitor pupils' achievements, progress and quality of teaching
- use data to analyse and evaluate performance
- generate and sustain discussion about teaching and learning
- sustain school improvement
- create school structures, systems and processes to enable all of this.

I was surprised to find that not all of these 'highly successful schools' that I visited had leaders who were 'learning centred' as described above. In fact in a few schools the head teachers did not actively 'generate and sustain discussion about teaching and learning', leaving this role to be done, if at all, by others. This is not to say the head teachers did not see it as important but it was apparent that in some schools there was no precedent for, and little pattern of, whole school dialogue around learning.

Supportive aspirational parents, competition amongst students and a positive focus on achievement quite clearly went a long way to explain some of the schools' successes and perhaps explain why some of the teaching could be quite pedestrian whilst academic results remained high. Here's a real paradox for those of us who say it's the quality of what happens in the classroom that is the most important factor in pupil learning.

In the 2006 NCSL publication *Seven Strong Claims about School Leadership,* Leithwood and others state – quite rightly as there is a vast body of evidence to support this – that 'school leadership is second only to classroom teaching as an influence on pupil learning'. What I found was that more challenging contexts required more imaginative and engaging approaches to learning. Enthusiastic, competitive and aspirational students bring challenges of their own but in most of the schools in this project poor behaviour was not an issue.

In one school the head teacher observed that he thought that 'a member of staff had chosen to take an interest in assessment for learning' and in another, with outstanding Ofsted ratings and highly successful academic results, the teaching and learning strand of the staff development enrichment programme was optional with 39 out of a total of 164 staff following the programme. In another school staff did not seem fully aware of what student engagement might mean: this despite there being a whole school 'drive' on the issue at the time. In another school, admittedly with high staff turnover, some staff had recently been appointed via an overseas agency without being seen before starting. Whilst it's easy to cherry-pick flaws, the point of interest is that all of these schools remain highly successful, some in the top 1 per cent of state schools in academic performance. Students achieve and get a good deal academically in these schools. The explanation for their successes is clearly not tied in to learning-centred leadership and a dialogue around learning as much as it may be or may have to be, in others.

For me, all of this was counter-intuitive to my own expectation and to the literature. Much of the leadership in schools focuses on learning centred leaders'. The 2004 NCSL publication on learning-centred leadership states that 'high performing and rapidly improving schools are characterised by learning centred leaders'.[8] I had expected to encounter passionate and universal debate and informed understanding of learning and the nature of the learner experience. What I found was a universal passion about achievement and progress but a very mixed picture around understanding of pedagogy and classroom practice. With some being genuinely leading edge and others, in what is a personal view, more akin to trailing edge.

Recommendation for leaders: generate and sustain whole school discussion about teaching and learning. Start by making it a standing agenda item on all school leadership and department meetings.

In the schools I visited I asked a number of questions around learning including how staff knew students were engaged with their learning and what constituted great classroom learning.

At Chafford, where lessons are of two hours duration and there is a whole school focus on creating more independence amongst learners, I was given a very detailed response from a teacher who was in middle leadership and four years in to teaching. She told me the ideal lesson was one where students were:

- passionate about, interested in and enjoying what they were doing
- mixed ability
- achieving from whatever their ability or starting point
- clear about outcomes
- developing and demonstrating independence
- looking to each other
- asking and answering great questions
- being challenged and challenging each other
- displaying higher order thinking skills.

The school had developed its own inventory of great learning using their own ideas and others taken from research or from schools. It was apparent that the widespread use of and reference to the school's inventory of learning features had shaped the thinking so that teachers no longer made reference to it as a document or strategy but had assimilated it into how they approached their own classroom practice.

Recommendation for leaders: review the quality of the learning experience against criteria that reflect the aspirations of the school. If you aspire to be world class in learning you have to go beyond the expectations of the inspectorate and the parent community.

In the core project schools I visited each was heavily oversubscribed. In some instances by more than tenfold! At Dixons Academy typically there were 1,000 applications for 165 places. None of the schools were now swimming against a tide of parental indifference, quite the reverse in fact. It had not always been that way. Some had worked hard to get themselves into this position. Now many of the schools I visited welcomed parents in the traditional roles of audience, recipients of reports or on invited consultative forums. Many actually preferred the parents at arm's length, talking up the concept of parental engagement whilst using systems, such as web-based information videos, to maintain an arm's length relationship. This was done with the best professional intent, typically 'we're the professionals, trust us but leave us to get on with the job'.

Imaginative practice to engage, educate and inform parents about their children's learning varied considerably across the schools. Again some of the practice I saw close up was inconsistent with the research literature:

> *Developing and sustaining effective partnerships between the home, the community and the school is, without question, the most important component of school improvement.*

> Alma Harris and Janet Goodall (2008)
> quoted in Harris, Andrew-Power and Goodall (2009)

In many schools there also appeared to be a competitive ethos amongst students to do well, which came from the students and their families, occasionally to the bemusement of staff. At Guru Nanak Sikh I was told that there were strong cultural pressures from outside the school driving performance. Amongst the things which were said during my visit supporting this were:

> *There's a real strong sense of family and community – in form time they talk all the time about family.*

> Head of ICT

> *It's such a close knit community here, we don't get misfits.*

> Assistant Head Teacher

43

The school's outstanding results have come as a by-product of family, com-
munity and faith – and if you asked them what would make them happy they'd
say 'getting a level 8', before adding,'You don't understand, sir, our parents are
Asian ...

Deputy Head Teacher

There's a lot of competitiveness and one-upmanship amongst students which
can also be demotivating as it's so public.

Head of Sixth Form

In at least half of the schools this competitive ethos spilled over amongst staff, particularly heads of subject who were often eager to be bettering their colleagues' exam results. Doreen Cronin at St Richard's described her staff as being 'quite competitive' adding, 'this quiet, friendly, healthy competition intensifies the drive for improvement in standards'.

At Haybridge, three of the middle leaders told me that there was very positive, healthy competition between departments but when a department was seen to be doing very well, for example in getting A students to be A* students, then through observations, meetings and insets, it was shared.[9] Stability amongst the staff helps here. A stable staff with lots of enthusers who are exposed to lots of opportunities for their own development and who are passionate about both subject and teaching was a prerequisite.

This healthy internal competition is once again something that doesn't seem to get picked up in the research literature but it was very clearly there and it was openly talked up amongst many of the staff I interviewed and quietly encouraged by leadership.

In the best schools the in-school variation is very small. Ask yourself, what's the difference between your best and worst department and what are you doing about it?

Recommendation for leaders: **be aware of, and try to channel, healthy internal competition especially between larger departments.**

It's become a leadership cliché to say that staffing is 'about getting the right people on the bus, sitting in the right seats and with the bus going in the right direction'. We hear it again and again. Stability amongst staff can mean 'low turbulence'. Students benefit from consistency and from the trust that comes with knowing their teachers.

Schools do what they can to attract talent and retain it. This includes:

- recruiting teaching talent over subject specialists
- early promotion
- additional responsibilities
- atomising responsibilities
- shared responsibilities
- parent-friendly contracts – start at 9.30 a.m. finish at 2.30 p.m.
- e-tutoring and mentoring from home
- paying staff to lead school in-service
- allowing staff to share their expertise beyond school – for example, individual staff with specialist IT skills worked with companies such as Adobe or Microsoft
- deploying staff for part of the week into a responsibility position in a partner school.

At Tudor Grange lots of posts are created with a mix of roles. The staff profile is very young and there is a real desire to 'grow their own'. Being a training school helps a great deal and the school leadership team take calculated risks on staffing. For example, with only one and a half jobs available for mathematicians and three outstanding candidates, they took all three.

Seven Kings pay for extra teachers in English and maths to allow for smaller groups to help improve speaking and listening and also have smaller groups around C/D border-lines. The appointment of a well-qualified and experienced librarian three years ago who, amongst other things, revamped the book club and initiated poetry readings and themed weeks, led to a 380 per cent increase in reading. At the time of my visit the school had 45 learning support assistants.

At Sandringham three advanced lead teacher posts were created for promising teachers not yet ready for the position of advanced skills teacher. Each was paid extra and given a three-year minimum contract and a responsibility for developing and improving an aspect of learning and teaching in the school. For example, conducting research, creating staff resources or delivering staff training in an area that related to the whole school learning and teaching focus. In addition, there was a termly voluntary secondment on to the leadership team for which anyone could apply. This has helped retain staff and maintain stability.

At St Angela's Ursuline School they employ around 10 to 12 gap year students each year. The gap year students are attached to departments, the sixth form or to year heads. Each student has an induction programme and over the year with the school builds a learning portfolio. They often return as exam invigilators and e-mentors. In the future some may well return as teachers.

At the Thomas Hardye School ex-students and gap year students are employed on learning support assistant rates as subject-specific coaches in maths, science, English and design technology. Because they have been in the situation of having to pass exams very recently they are both coach and role model to the sixth formers.

With every appointment, involve the appropriate people. Some head teachers don't let the head of English become involved in appointing an NQT in English! Don't appoint if you know it's wrong. There is always a solution eventually! It helps if you can be really flexible on contracts; for example, in some schools it's possible for a contract that is 9.30 a.m. to 2.30 p.m., allowing people to miss last lesson and pick up their young children.

Recommendation for leaders: be prepared to be creative to recruit and retain great talent. Brilliant teachers don't often come by so take them when they come your way and find the posts or the contracts to do so.

Keep what's already good and works well! If you have excellent teachers in one subject area don't compromise their strengths by attempting to introduce something new that may be vulnerable because of weak teaching. It should be right for the students but a broad offer is not the answer to everything. A child is far better getting a C in a subject with a great teacher than U in, for example, health and social care where you couldn't appoint so made the PE teacher teach it!

If you have excess staff in a specialist area like PE or music, write to all the primary schools and ask if they want to invest in half a day a week. Similarly if you are short could the local secondary school help out?

Be creative about appointing staff if you are in an area where it is really hard to get teachers. If you find two brilliant history teachers and can't find a geography teacher swop the curriculum round for a year and give KS3 less geography. There are lots of history teachers out there so advertise for history/English if you can't find English teachers. A good history teacher with a Year 7 class is infinitely preferable to an agency teacher who is hopeless and likely to leave at the end of term!

Look elsewhere for inspiration regarding recruiting, retaining and refreshing staff. The Teach First initiative aims to put young talent into some of the most challenging school contexts. It has a reverse motivational hook. It challenges young graduates to defer going into highly paid jobs in places like the city and instead go into some of the maintained schools which are to be found in inner cities. It's a curious proposition. If you're good enough we'll accept you so you can experience what it's like at the edge of your comfort zone. The message is: do something worthwhile, become part of an elite. As a selling proposition it's brilliant. Corporate employers are lining up to sponsor the programme. Teach First is also exceptionally good at maintaining the sense of being part of a young dynamic team driven by a moral purpose. Again, schools can learn from this.

It seems to work. Researchers were commissioned by the charity to look at how well the programme was doing and how it could be improved. After analysing data and conducting interviews in 87 Teach First schools and 87 comparable secondary schools, and with 848 teachers across England, the team from Manchester University found a significant correlation between participation in Teach First and improved pupil achievement one to two years after the teachers start at the school.[10]

Teach First selects by identifying the competencies for those recruited onto its programme. They have exacting standards and it is not a shoo-in to get onto the programme.

The competencies required from Teach First teachers

After minimum academic requirements, selection is based on one's ability to demonstrate relevant subject knowledge and the following competencies:

Humility, respect and empathy – *Always respects and values others*

Interaction – *Adapts communication style to work well with others, a great team player*

Knowledge – *Has a passion for their subject and uses it to make a difference and help us achieve our mission*

Leadership – *Leads the way, constantly raising the bar to make success happen*

Planning and organising – *Works efficiently and effectively to deliver success*

Problem solving – *A considered approach, works smart to come up with the best solutions*

Resilience – *Loves a challenge and keeps going to overcome them*

Self-evaluation – *Knows strengths.*

This model, which recruits on the basis of potential, looking first at the personal qualities of the individual rather than their experience or qualifications, is something schools may like to adapt. It's not a perfect model. There's a glaring omission in that it does not mention learning, substituting a 'passion for their subject' rather than a passion for learning and what it may offer. Nor, in this checklist, does it mention any moral impera- tive for the role of the teacher in transforming lives. That said it offers a useful prompt to help schools think about locating talent.

Recommendation for leaders: look at the criteria against which you recruit young teachers and learning support assistants. Is it too restrictive? Can you design a better alternative?

4. Staying the course

Shortly after I survived a vote of no confidence, we were given notice to improve. At that point I felt my time had come – turned out to be a call to action!

Chris Tomlinson, Head Teacher, Chafford Hundred Campus

I personally interviewed lots of individuals in assembling this book. Outside of school leadership teams, there were 37 middle leaders and 25 recently qualified or 'new' teachers who were each spoken to for at least 45 minutes. Although staff were put forward by the host school they were chosen against my broad criteria and their availability on the day, rather than any public relations skills. Of the 62 individuals interviewed there was not a single instance of anyone being critical of the school leadership teams or of the head teacher. I was taken aback. Admittedly I didn't push for negative views, but all interviewees were candid and honest.

It was refreshing that staff were so positive with many volunteering examples of moments, behaviours or interventions that had carried significance for them. At St Richard's Catholic College, an 11–16 school of over 1,000 students, I was told that the principal knew all the children's names; at Haybridge staff told me they believed the head teacher paid for their staff celebrations from her own money; at Thornden it had been essential that others were seen to be good enough to step into the head teacher's shoes when he had been absent through illness; at Dixons a member of staff was close to tears when describing how the head teacher had stuck by her during a protracted illness. Again and again in every one of the schools visited there was a clear appreciation for the 'human' side of leadership.

It can be no more than an impression, and each of the leadership styles I encountered inevitably reflected the context of the school and the personality of the head teachers I spoke to, but there was a 'steeliness' about each. At St Richard's Catholic College, I was taken by the way in which the principal, Doreen Cronin, an unassuming woman, described how they would 'chase and chase' students, never giving up on them. Reconciliation was important, there was lots and lots of starting again, but so too were the rules: 'Never reject any child – I've got some children who will be on bail half their lives but they stick to the rules when they're here.' When she said this you could tell by the tone in her voice she meant it!

It has become customary to deride the concept of the hero leader or 'lone fixer' but in truth the behaviours that were described to me as cementing loyalty or creating 'reciprocation' were accumulations of small, quietly *heroic* behaviours.

Recommendation for leaders: **put people before policies. Coercive, policy-driven leadership gets you compliance whilst supportive, policy-aware leadership gets you loyalty.**

In the schools that formed the core research for this book, the 15 SSAT picks and my 5 outliers, experience as a head teacher ranged from one instance of 23 years to another of less than 23 weeks. Typically the head teacher was experienced, with 8 to 12 years as a head teacher, in some cases more, and in some cases experience of being a head teacher in more than one school.

Ten of those interviewed had recent experience of leading another school either as an executive head teacher or as a temporary arrangement to help a school in difficulty. I worked out that the collective head teacher experience amongst those in the 20 schools was around 195 years. I was too polite to confirm this by actually asking, but looking at my list now, 11 of the head teachers will be of retirement age within the next six years.

Few of the schools, with one notable exception, had placed significant numbers of new head teachers into the wider system directly from their staff. This is a system issue. The model in most of these schools, though again not all, was to retain talent by offering new roles and responsibilities. In several schools there were deputy head teachers who were long serving and remaining in post. This offered stability, continuity and experience. This was seen as a considerable strength in many schools whilst in others it posed a challenge for developing the wider leadership team, especially assistant head teachers coming through.

Recommendation for leaders: **create development opportunities by widening the school leadership team, breaking down larger responsibilities and creating new roles.**

In only two instances was the head teacher I interviewed a relatively recent – i.e. less than five years – appointment from outside the school. Stability was a noticeable feature of the school leadership teams. In eight of the schools the incumbent head teacher had been appointed from within, having spent significant time as a deputy.

In some cases the predecessor head teacher had broken the ground either without or in most cases with, the now head teacher as deputy. In five of the schools the predecessor head teacher had been a nationally known figure, esteemed for changing the circumstances of the school and therefore inevitably a hard act to follow. This is a dilemma not unprecedented in other walks of life, notably public office, sport and business, but a relatively new phenomenon for education, especially if your predecessor is moving on to an even more prominent headship or public role. In each case the incumbent head teacher I interviewed had embraced the challenge, protecting the legacy whilst bringing a very different leadership style.

At one of the schools I visited, the head of science told me that the 'previous head teacher had a close control ethos which took us forward but could never have unleashed our creativity'. He went on to add, 'The new head teacher let the genie out of the bottle – with tight values and loose control: it took us from good to outstanding.'

At another school, the head teacher described his predecessor as charismatic but his arrival was like 'the sudden appearance of storm troopers in the corridors'. He went on to describe how in the late 1980s the five A–C were the worst in the county and the staff were often quietly, and occasionally openly, subversive. For three years the predecessor head, who was described as having had a hugely top-down management style, 'wrestled control back from the students and imposed accountability on the staff. He was really smart. He had made everyone believe they could be the best school in the country but he also realised that his particular leadership style wasn't right to take them there.'

A new senior team brought with it a change of style and emphasis: 'We introduced internal self-inspection, quality standards, target-setting, a simpler curriculum, a strong management structure, higher levels of accountability and we invested really heavily in extracurricular provision. It worked!'

Recommendation for leaders: protect the legacy whilst finding your own style.

We know more and more about models of leadership and the importance of 'distributed' leadership and shared responsibility. In the schools I visited I saw very different models of leadership. From this short survey there is no one model that emerges as the norm.

Most, but not all, schools had large leadership teams with flat structures and five to eight people with leadership responsibilities. From within this group there was often a smaller group upon whom most of the day-to-day responsibilities lay.

However, a small cohort of these successful schools did not seem to have read the literature on distributed leadership. Of the schools that were visited, three of twenty had what could be described as traditional senior management structures of head teacher or principal and two or three deputies. In these schools it appeared that most decision making and authority resided within this group. In each case they were highly regarded by the staff I spoke to but in these schools I found little evidence of key decisions being pushed down.

Some of the language used in the interviews veered towards the reverential. One middle leader talked of being 'a strong candidate for a management course'. Another talked about being nervous when going to the head teacher to explain a 'slight overspend in the departmental budget'. Relationships were more formal in these three schools. In one, fortnightly review meetings with the line manager from the school leadership team would have a formal agenda with what were described as 'set questions'. In the remainder of the schools the leadership models encountered were less concentrated on a powerful group.

In *Seven Strong Claims about School Leadership*, it states that leadership 'acts as a catalyst allowing other good things to happen'. That was certainly the case in many of the schools but the individuals concerned and the contexts in which they found themselves were so different that 'getting leadership right' meant very different things. If we take the 'seven strong claims' and apply them to our schools we can highlight some similarities and some significant differences.

Claim one

School leadership is second only to classroom teaching as an influence on pupil learning. Whilst not all schools had what Ofsted would call outstanding teaching and learning, all the schools had strong, highly visible and well-regarded leadership. Succession, and planning for succession, was a successful feature in most of the schools albeit from within. However in one, finding a successor had been so problematic that the incumbent head teacher had been persuaded to stay on three times.

Claim two

Almost all successful leaders draw on the same repertoire of basic leadership practices. All head teachers built a vision around core purpose or maintained a vision or supplanted a previous vision with an improved equivalent. All set high standards. Some seemed to be more proactive in setting a direction for the school than others. Most integrated the functional with the personal – developing, supporting and challenging staff to achieve agreed goals. Staff consistently reported feeling valued and that their job was worthwhile.

Claim three

The ways in which leaders apply these basic leadership practices – not the practices themselves – demonstrate responsiveness to, rather than dictation by, the contexts in which they work. Leadership practices were varied by context. Some head teachers articulated how they'd had to adopt a style in the early phases of their leadership and were now changing, usually for more to less control. Others contrasted the necessary differences in their 'style' with their predecessor. Some saw themselves as practitioner leaders, other as strategic leaders. Some were collegiate and consulted widely. A few, including those described above as more traditional, ran a small 'cabinet' of trusted leadership peers.

Claim four

School leaders improve teaching and learning indirectly and most powerfully through their influence on staff motivation, commitment and working conditions. No direct mention was made during interviews of any leadership responsibility to implement national strategies or ensure staff were up to date in the content knowledge related to their subject. Many talked of the importance of staying close to exam board requirements so were attuned to the need for the school to be well positioned in understanding what should be taught and how it would be tested. All school leadership teams were aware of the need to keep abreast of modern learning methods and to update pedagogy. Although some did this very well, others did not give it the whole school status the literature suggests it deserves. Most leadership teams were clear that their role was to clear the way for staff to plan, deliver, evaluate and improve student learning experiences.

Claim five

School leadership has a greater influence on schools and students when it is widely distributed. In schools which had very strong linear structures with very large departments it was clear that whole school dialogue and shared problem solving around learning with shared approaches to aspects of learning – for example, lesson planning, learning methods, assessment techniques, questioning strategies, classroom observation – was more problematic. In a few instances this was more marked because the middle leaders did not have significant autonomy.

Claim six

Some patterns of distribution are more effective than others. I found no examples of laissez-faire forms of leadership. In many instances there was talk of setting people free or of having 'tight values but loose control' but this was not in an immature stage of development for the school, nor was it ill informed. The head teachers knew what they wanted.

Claim 7

A small handful of personal traits explains a high proportion of the variation in leadership effectiveness. The head teacher and leadership teams interviewed all operated out of a set of strongly held convictions. Most, though not all, were strongly defensive of their autonomy from 'outside' agencies including the local authority. One school team talked of their obligation to the wider community of schools and how that had shaped their thinking over academy status. Another valued its place as a local authority comprehensive. Most were tiger-ish in their defence of staff from unwanted pressures, their pursuit of core purpose as they perceived it and their commitment to do the best, however that was defined, for their students.

Recommendation for leaders: **your leadership practices and the leadership structures you put in place should not be set in stone or determined by one model of success. However, there are robust claims about getting leadership right. These are worth pursuing.**

A very high percentage of head teachers in English schools are over the age of 50. Many will retire or seek to retire, in the next few years. High performing schools owe it to the system to continue to develop talented young leaders and feed them into the system. Not enough are doing so.

When appointing staff to middle leadership positions, St John the Baptist School commits to getting the person ready for a deputy head teacher position within two years. They say so at interview. Succession planning is not built into the planning cycle at the school, nor is it at the forefront of thinking, but in 15 years there have been 15 head teachers emerge from St John the Baptist School with 12 of those appointed directly. The school is adding exceptional value to the system. How has this come about?

There is a high turnover of staff at the school but there is an equally strong conviction that those who leave will be replaced by others who are equally as good. Staff are regularly asked about what the school can do to help them be even better at their job. Personal well-being targets feature in every performance management plan. The school does what it can to alleviate some of those personal burdens that might constrain performance: they have a staff ironing service, collective membership of a health club, online shopping, on-site car MOT. The commitment is to free staff to do their jobs. Promoted posts are created to smooth the way for talent to grow. Where possible, staff are employed on their ability to teach and their potential, not on their subject specialism or their qualifications. Responsibility is pushed down though the head teacher is quick to admit that an experienced core has been essential. The concept is to identify talent and develop it at every opportunity:

- Every second week the school leadership team meeting is a development meeting which focuses on such things as: timetabling, how to manage a budget, leadership styles.

- All staff are encouraged to visit other schools to benchmark and in doing so are sent in pairs. They talk about school improvement all the way there and all the way back!

- Any member of staff attending a whole school course reports back in a written summary so that all benefit.

- There is 360-degree appraisal for all senior leadership team (SLT) members with three things to do to improve.

- There is flexibility about who is on the SLT with a rolling programme of staff coming on to gain experience and a whole school perspective.

- Unnecessary paperwork, including policy documents, are required to be kept to a minimum, often at the expense of following national initiatives.

- Performance evaluation is fundamental to everything they do but it is done with a light touch – what went well (WWW) and even better if (EBI).

Recommendation for leaders: **make every second school leadership team meeting a development meeting.**

5. Saying no to peripherals

For us, Sewa – selfless service – is at the core of what we do.

Rajinder Sandhu, Head Teacher, Guru Nanak Sikh School

More is not necessarily better. As some quote – or perhaps misquote – Albert Einstein, 'Doing the same thing again and again and expecting a different result is a form of insanity.' Adding more approaches, initiatives, requirements, checks or balances without removing what went before can lead to discord. At Walthamstow I was told by one of the middle leaders that 'chasing initiatives disunites staff'.

Rob Sykes, head teacher of Thornden, told me that they pick very few initiatives: 'We are often concerned that some schools are advised to burden themselves with a tragic amount of "stuff" which saps the energy of the staff.'

Delia Smith, writing in 2009 as the then head teacher of St Angela's Ursuline School, pointed out that the investment of the leaders' and the institution's time in any 'other agenda' should be proportional to the value it offers to the students, pointing out 'the tail should never wag the dog'.

This is especially the case with learning and teaching. Here's a list of some of the approaches to learning and teaching I've come across in visiting secondary schools in England in the last year:

Accelerated Learning
Accelerated Reader
Assertive Mentoring
Assessment for Learning
Building Learning Power
Cognitive Behavioural Therapy
Co-operative Structures
Critical Skills
Emotional Intelligence
Engaging Minds
Enquiry-Based Learning
Five Minds for the Future
Habits of Mind

Heartmath

Higher Order Thinking Skills

Intensive Interventions

Learning Futures

Learning to Learn

Motivational Interviewing

Opening Minds

Peer Mentoring

Pennsylvania Resilience Programme

Personal Learning and Thinking Skills

Philosophy for Children

Project-Based Learning

Reading Recovery

Reciprocal Teaching

Restorative Justice

Skills for Learning and Leading

Social and Emotional Aspects of Learning

Student Voice

Talking to Learn

Thinking Actively in a Social Context (TASC)

Structure of Observed Learning Outcome (SOLO) taxonomy

Teacher Effectiveness Enhancement Programme (TEEP)

Thinking Schools

Thinking through School Project

Vivo Rewards

This is just a snapshot of some of the approaches I've seen being used in schools, in mixed combinations and with mixed success, over the last year. If it looks like a dog's dinner then that's how it can feel to a visitor looking in on schools that have assembled their approach piecemeal. It can be really difficult for schools to scan the horizon and know where to place their efforts. Inspiration doesn't always come from within. Sometimes the complexity is exaggerated by a misguided attempt to replicate what's been successful elsewhere.

Schools like Cramlington Learning Village have had hundreds of visitors from around the globe come to look at their innovative approaches to learning and their use of technology to support and extend learning. In addition, they have an annual national conference with close to 200 visitors taking part in an informative, shared learning experience. Cramlington Learning Village is more than ten years down this route and has had innovative approaches to learning constantly evolving over that time. For some schools to try and copy and paste the present Cramlington Learning Village approach is not a fruitful investment. For schools that may be teetering on the point of failure, getting the basics right and in place is more about abandoning unhelpful activity than searching for the next possibility. In this regard there is a great deal to be said for proximal development – finding and replicating the journey rather than its destination. The schools that are a year or two further on may contain a great deal worth replicating.

Recommendation for leaders: focus down on what matters – planning, delivering, evaluating and improving quality learning experiences for your students.

> *Tight values, loose control: get the values right, get good people, find opportunities and let it go.*
>
> Stephen Munday, Head Teacher, Comberton Village College

Some schools are overstretched by a lack of focus on what works and what can serve their core purpose. The better schools shape their own agendas. The school leadership team at Seven Kings told me, 'We do things to our own agenda and being in the outstanding category allows us to do so.' At Sandringham I was told, 'We follow what's right for us and do so together.'

Mike Griffiths says of Northampton School for Boys, 'We aren't trailblazers, it's often better to be in the group just behind, but we feel we are in the best position to decide what's best for our students. Ultimately if you don't believe in doing something then don't do it.' At the school there is a simple curriculum offer that allows a strong line management structure with clear accountability and setting enabled by a simpler curriculum choice. The school has no or very few resits and no early entry. The argument put to me was what's the point of getting an early C if by continuing you can get an A*. It was pointed out to me that the school doesn't believe in work experience and so has never done it. They don't, in their words, do mechanistic 'three strikes and you're out' type behaviour strategies. Nor do they write down 'aims and all that stuff' and that perhaps after 12 years of continuous improvement it may be that they are about to plateau! Refreshingly honest – and as was pointed out, it's about sticking to the knitting! As I left the head teacher he gave me a copy of the summary of the three-year school improvement plan: two sides of A4 (admittedly landscape not portrait).

Recommendation for leaders: give as much attention to identifying and abandoning existing unhelpful practices as to searching for emerging innovation.

6. Exacting self-scrutiny

We took a more disciplined approach to aspiration and removed the overbearing pastoral dimension to learning support.

Mike Griffiths, Head Teacher, Northampton School for Boys

Who are the leaders in your school? What are the everyday behaviours you want from these leaders? At Abraham Guest School, a school that sits outside of the research project, the arrival of a new head teacher coincided with the move to a new build about one mile away from the original site. In the old building, a 1960s comprehensive, the corridors were many and narrow; the stairways were congested and there were lots of little hideaways and unobserved spaces for students to conceal themselves. Staff were constantly vigilant and many of the behavioural issues in the old building emerged from overcrowding and the turmoil it can generate. When the students arrived at the more spacious building, where there were open spaces, high walls, curved surfaces and a boulevard feel to the main part of the school, many of the behavioural issues disappeared. Students had responded to the environment. In fact in some of the meeting areas it appeared as though the students didn't know how to traverse the larger open spaces, appearing very self-conscious as they did so.

Just as the students had to adapt and change their relationship with the space so too did their teachers, some doing so better than others. For some of the staff the old ways and the old thinking were difficult to shrug off. 'Where will I put my filing cabinet?' may seem an irrelevance to some when you are being asked to teach in a new and custom-built, multi-functional space with state-of-the-art technologies. But it's hard to shift old thinking. So it was apposite for the new head teacher, Paul Bousefield, to ask his colleagues to review the leadership behaviours across the school.

They worked together in an off-site facilitated session running over 24 hours that went through the processes below. The desired outcome was an agreed framework of leader behaviours that would be used in the school. Each stage had the team working in three separate groups, then coming together to share similarities and differences. At each stage an agreed set of outcomes led into the subsequent stage:

- agree our core purpose as a school community
- revisit our existing mission statement, motto and values to see if they adequately reflect our core purpose

- define what great leader behaviours are
- write those behaviours up as seven generic behaviours each of which can be adapted for other leader roles, e.g. middle leader, student leader
- from each heading break it down into three characteristics, which will be our framework and against which we will evaluate our performance
- commit to exhibiting the behaviours from the next school day
- use our next whole team meeting to examine how we are doing and build in space at all subsequent meetings to explore an aspect of the framework
- commit to the behaviours in all our documentation.

From the session the following commitment emerged: Leaders at Abraham Guest School are team players who strive to enhance the life chances of students and are:

- Solution focused
- Positive
- Visible
- Challenging
- Aware of self and others
- Strategic
- Innovative.

This then became the leadership behaviours framework:

- Solution focused
  - Generates outcomes which move the organisation on
  - Shares information in a productive, timely way
  - Consults and empowers others to agree shared steps to success.
- Positive
  - Consciously positive verbal and non-verbal communication
  - Actively promoting the same shared message
  - Builds relationships in a calm, considered professional way.

- Visible

  - Is seen around school and in classrooms

  - Demonstrates responsibility by taking an enthusiastic lead on a whole school issue

  - Has a high profile presence in the school and wider community.

- Challenging

  - Asks searching questions

  - Can assume the role of a critical friend

  - Insists on accountability and provides evidence-based feedback.

- Aware of self and others

  - Reflects on the intent behind behaviours

  - Understands, interprets and responds to one's own strengths and weaknesses and those of others

  - Chooses appropriate methods of communication and behaviours.

- Strategic

  - Aware of the bigger picture and the factors which shape it

  - Identify and prioritise key areas for development

  - Anticipate and balance short, medium and long-term demands.

- Innovative

  - Open-minded and willing to consider a range of alternatives

  - Appreciate and supportive of original thinking

  - Makes professional judgements on the worth of innovation.

In the NCSL publication *Everyone a Leader* (2007b) it suggests that there are essentials of leadership that transcend individual contexts. It adds that the quality of leadership development at all levels will be determined by the culture, ethos, attitudes and disposition of the school. In leadership learning, one of four core areas of development, *Everyone a Leader* suggests that all staff can benefit from an exploration of their leadership qualities and aspirations. It talks of using performance management to recognise their leadership potential and develop leadership and the language of leadership across the school.

The beauty of the list above is that it was generated by the very people charged to shift their behaviours. It starts from individual behaviours that can then be modelled and replicated across the school. The next task would be to identify how each behaviour impacts on students.

Recommendation for leaders: identify the generic leader behaviours you wish to see modelled across the whole school community and, starting with the school leadership team, evaluate their impact.

How are we doing? What could we do better? What should we do more of? What should we do less of? What should we abandon? All good questions but without the views of all those involved, *the stakeholders*, they are not questions to which you can provide purposeful answers.

Quality assurance differs from quality control. The former is about ensuring your systems have integrity built into them and so a high standard is assured when the system operates as it should. Assurance relies on lots of performance feedback on what's working and what needs to be changed. The latter is about bringing the human input into line with the system. Control relies on lots of checks to ensure compliance and when problems arise it's often the human who has not met the standard. Better for schools to focus on quality assurance but those systems need to have underpinning controls.

As I write, the *Daily Telegraph* has just gleefully published a copy of a report sent to a parent from a Lincolnshire secondary school containing 14 spelling errors.[11] The head teacher offered an apology and the newspaper put it alongside the school's website claim to be a 'trailblazing' institution. The report was sent directly from the teacher by email and not checked. The consequence? Local and, sadly, national notoriety. The answer? Quality assurance systems within which are a number of checks along the way: proofread by teacher, checked by middle leader, sampled by head teacher.

You don't want your feedback through the national press so ensure that you regularly obtain it from your staff, students, parents and others with whom you work. Identify what are the core 'services' you must provide and think how you might begin to quality assure these services. Ask yourself what a quality experience might be in the following situations:

- A student arriving at school late

- The catering staff dealing with students

- A parent receiving a letter from school

- The site management team stacking chairs

- A parent making an appointment with the school

- Students on placement

- Parents being told their son is excluded

- A visitor walking around the site for the first time

- The trainer leading your twilight session on behaviour management

- Prospective parents attending an open evening

- Students waiting for lunch

- New staff settling in

- A visitor phoning to seek directions

- Applicants emailing for job details

- Students who are banned from the play areas because it's raining

- A member of the cleaning staff who has a bereavement

- Staff wanting to stay late

- A child whose mobile phone has been stolen.

At St John the Baptist School the head teacher blocks time to interview every Year 11 student with their parent or parents. At Haybridge it is with Year 10. They are asked about their learning and their experience, what's gone well and what could be done better. Caroline Hoddinott explains she is always looking to fine-tune and improve. Parent consultation evenings at St John the Baptist allow head teacher Ani Magill an opportunity to ask parents for short written feedback on an easy-to-complete postcard. The outcomes are analysed and then later fed back to parents using a 'You said, We did' summary, which is placed on the website. Both these schools have a 360-degree feedback system in place for each member of the school leadership team and use this to further develop quality assurance.

Recommendation for leaders: ensure you have a quality assurance system in place to ensure that for all stakeholders the school 'experience' is positive.

High performing schools are, as one head teacher put it, 'bang on the data'. However, the data needs to be filtered so that it does not overwhelm and humanised so that we talk students rather than stats. At St John the Baptist School the advice was 'Don't flood staff with data. They don't look at it and so won't use the important stuff. Provide the grade the student should get and make everything else available online if staff want it. Use strategies that communicate how students are performing. For example, "Traffic Lights" to show where students are achieving above, on or below their target.'

At Walthamstow School for Girls, head teacher Rachel Macfarlane said that data analysis was one of the few things she changed on arrival at the school. She wanted staff to be enabled to analyse in more depth and to be able to drill down and look at every child and be able to track their progress easily, regularly and consistently. She employed a data manager, insisted that targets have to be upper quartile or above and looked carefully at levels of progress from KS2.

At another school, departmental meetings often have pictures of under-achieving students to remind the team about who they are, what interventions are in place, what progress has been made as a consequence and what happens next. It's then followed up.

Recommendation for leaders: put the most relevant student performance data into the hands of those who need it most, at the right time and in the most accessible format.

Two:
The trapeze – teachers performing

Performing on the trapeze was so risky, even the doubles had doubles.

Tony Curtis, on the 1956 film *Trapeze*

Teacher talk

The words and phrases most used by teachers in our interviews:

7. Build from the BASICS

Relationships are everything – you have to build on solid foundations.

History Teacher, Emmanuel College

Many years ago a teacher told me that in his school each classroom had an A4 frame, which was open at the top and mounted alongside the door. Inside the frame the teacher could slip a sheet of paper, which contained any items thought appropriate for the incoming class to know about. He made it his business to refresh it regularly and used to put things in there about what he had been reading; the television programmes he liked; music he liked or disliked; jokes he'd heard; and things he was looking forward to. He said that the frame changed his relationship for the better with each and every class. From being a new and unknown teacher he quickly became accepted.

Learning at its very best is about taking risks and going beyond one's comfort zone. Great learning environments are those where personal challenge can extend the comfort zone without being undermined by overwhelming levels of anxiety. In high challenge environments with a big emphasis on performance and performance outcomes there can be considerable inhibitions on risk taking. Students play safe. In high challenge environments with a big emphasis on learning and learning outcomes it's easier to give it a go. Students accept risk.

With high anxiety environments, whether it's a cage or a classroom, we get the release of unhelpful stress-related chemicals designed to heighten awareness of potential predators and speed our quick escape! These are the worst conditions for a learner! High levels of uncertainty, poor or no levels of choice, physical inhibition, intense and extended focus on one set of stimuli – all contribute to a raising of the stress threshold. Put any mammal in this state for too long and you get the classic survival behaviours: fight, flight, freeze and flock. Your students have the potential to do just this. Once there, as a classroom teacher it's the point of no return!

Positive relationships, feeling safe, being treated as an individual, being challenged, experiencing structure, clarity of purpose, consistency of response, involvement in decision making, variety in learning and feeling good about oneself all contribute to getting the basics in place. A well-grooved formula for creating a safe learning environment in which learners will be more prepared to take some personal risks in learning is described in the acronym BASICS:

- Belonging – learners are known, recognised and feel part of the class or school community

- Aspiration – learners can measure progress towards outcomes of their choosing

- Safety – learners are free from physical or psychological intimidation

- Identity – learners are treated as autonomous individuals and are encouraged to express their individuality

- Challenge – learners are challenged and give task-related feedback in support of coping with that challenge

- Success – successful learner behaviours are captured, reinforced and celebrated.

Recommendation for teachers: get the basics in place, build positive relationships and create high challenge low stress classrooms.

Staff here go above and beyond the call of duty – many are still here at 8 at night, and at 7.30 in the morning there are cars in the car park.

Middle Leaders, Haybridge School

I often ask of long-serving staff if they ever have occasion to meet ex-pupils who had left many years before and for whom school could easily be distant and all but forgotten. What gets remembered and what's filtered out and forgotten? The things that are forgotten are the worksheets, the marking, test scores, levels, homework, exonerations about behaviour, guidance on shirts, ties and haircuts, detentions and lesson objectives. The minutiae of school life that consumes so much of your time is forgotten and what gets remembered are the hours spent freezing on Dartmoor; the day you were left behind on the bus coming back from the Somme; the football team that went a season unbeaten; the standing ovation after the brass band competition in the Town Hall; the day you brought in cakes because it was your birthday; the day the mouse escaped in the classroom. The teachers who go the extra mile benefit from what psychologists call reciprocation or mutual loyalty. The impact of the extra mile shouldn't be underestimated. Whether it's formal or informal, conventional or unconventional, it makes a difference.

Mike Griffiths, head teacher at Northampton School for Boys, believes that the school's huge extracurricular programme is the biggest driver of success. They benefit from a virtuous circle as staff go 'above and beyond' the call of duty. The ethos is one of high participation with lots of emphasis on sport, performing arts, especially theatre and music, and overseas trips. There are 14 different bands, orchestras or groups and 7 peripatetic groups. Older students and alumni mentor younger talent, especially in music. All over-seas trips take place in holiday time. As a consequence of the students seeing staff in different roles beyond the classroom, forming relationships that sit outside academic work and being aware of the effort staff put in, it's felt that boys are more 'biddable'. Mike Griffiths puts it this way: 'there is a prevailing ethos that boys can get on, which can mean that many of our lessons are not as dynamic as perhaps we'd like. Staff here don't move on, they just don't want to go. It's not a bad thing, it's a loyalty thing.'

A young teacher at Northampton School for Boys commented that when he ran a Year 10 football team he started to notice a benefit and so he started to run a music fanzine: 'Music and sport are the places where difficult boys find an outlet and the benefits feed in, especially for boys who have problems with authority.'

Recommendation for teachers: find opportunities for your students to see you in a different light. Take a responsibility outside of the classroom.

One-to-one mentoring took place in most of the schools visited. It varied in those who were mentored, who it was who did the mentoring, when it occurred and how it occurred.

At the Thomas Hardye School, mentoring took a number of forms. The school has adopted motivational interviewing techniques to help staff work particularly with stu-dents who are having difficulties seeing the point of schooling. Often these students have oppositional behaviours so do not always respond to the predictable entreaties. Motivational interviewing uses the techniques described by the acronym OARS: (1) Open-ended questions, (2) Affirmations, (3) Reflective listening and (4) Summaries. The power of this technique is that it leads the students to arrive at their own conclusions and so is more 'motivational'. Students leave having set their own goals and secured a plan to deliver their goals.

Gap year students from Thomas Hardye are also used as subject-specific coaches in maths, science, English and design because they have been in the situation very re-cently, come through, succeeded and are now in an advantageous position: they are both coach and role model.

At St Angela's, peer mentoring involved volunteers from Years 10 and 11. Twelve stu-dents were selected and then trained. In the last year 58 students were seen by peer mentors in a 'drop in and talk' system. Mentoring in the sixth form takes two forms – mentoring as enrichment, and mentoring as an intervention. In the former it's the sixth formers who are doing the mentoring and in the latter they are being mentored. Year 11 students who are not currently attached to any support systems, typically about 40, are targeted for mentoring. Each mentor has a job description, receives training, meets with other mentors to share techniques and then is carefully matched with a Year 11 student. Mentees are set weekly targets and meet during school time. Typical topics to cover would include: updating revision timetables, practising past paper questions, completion of coursework, time management, focusing on specific subjects. Sixth formers also mentor form groups lower down the school.

At Walthamstow, staff mentor 150 of the 180 girls in who are in Year 11 and those Year 10s who staff believe would derive most benefit or who may be at risk. Lots of support staff including school administration staff, site managers and laboratory technicians are involved as mentors and fulfil the role exceptionally well.

Recommendation for teachers: develop the skills of mentoring, particularly the skills of building and maintaining rapport, asking good questions and listening.

8. Relentless optimism

Underachievement is immediately challenged, achievement is immediately celebrated.

Geography Teacher, Seven Kings School

The one thing that can make the most difference in student success in your classroom is their self-concept. How do they see themselves? When they were 4 years of age did they enjoy doing the one jigsaw again and again, basking in the glory of their parents' praise, or did they like doing different jigsaws, struggling a little but getting there in the end? Are they bound up in themselves and their own innate abilities, or are they shaped by tasks and their ability to adjust to a challenge?

Just as schools have stories to tell which help them articulate their journey so too does an individual. We justify everyday behaviours, decisions large and small, results of tests and exams, and they become our story. The story could be one of 'I had an off day when I sat the exam, I would have passed otherwise' or equally 'I failed, it was my fault, I just didn't put in the hours'. Ultimately, it's the same outcome but the stories explaining it are worlds apart. For a student attributing success or failure to factors over which they have no control is the ultimate debilitation. It's a dead end. For a student able to accept responsibility for factors over which they have control is the launch pad to success.

To which factors do your students attribute their successes and failures? Factors that are out of their control? Or factors within their control? The difference is huge. Optimism for its own sake, being cheery whatever comes your way, is not a lot of use. The self-help and self-esteem movements that washed over the Atlantic to the UK in the mid-1980s did our schools and teachers a disservice when overlooking the crucial importance of challenge in building belief. If you doubt this, try to change behaviour through a collage, an illustrated family tree, a coat of arms or a mantra. It doesn't work! Exposing the individual to challenge is the missing dimension. But, having said that, experiencing miserable failure or easy success does little to build what we'll call self-efficacy. It's how we learn to make sense of the experience and subsequently to position the narrative around the experience which makes the long-term difference.

Recommendation for teachers: be very aware of how your students frame success and failure. Encourage them to be incremental and focus on small performance improvements.

No child is given a target below a C – what would be the point of that?

Middle Leader, Tudor Grange School

At the Thomas Hardye School in Dorchester the head teacher, Iain Melvin, is fond of using the term *relentless optimism* and sees it as a mantra for the school. Talking of the need for a positive attitude he claims the 'single limiting factor on student achievement is teacher imagination'. Amongst the things he describes as important in keeping optimism relentless at Thomas Hardye are:

- making a big school seem like a small school by knowing the students and drilling down into the data

- rewarding initiative – both staff and students

- artefacts and visual reminders related to personal achievements

- head teacher presence around the school

- developing people whilst holding them to account

- motivational interviewing and one-to-one mentoring

- involving parents

- rigour throughout.

One-to-one interviewing is a feature of the school. All teachers are timetabled for at least one lesson each week to see three students. The head teacher sees ten different students once fortnightly and has them rate their lessons out of ten.

At Guru Nanak Sikh the head teacher sees a different group of students every Friday and asks a similar question. Knowing who the students are and what they need is essential and can be motivational.

A formula for motivation, which you may find useful, is that it equals *opportunity* plus *expectancy* times *value*.

Opportunity is key. A student may be given the opportunity to take part in the school production, play for a team, go on a field trip or be entered early for an exam. There is something about scarcity and about accessing a resource or an experience or a moment that is not available to everyone that releases adrenaline. As soon as the student knows he or she is in then the adrenaline follows. Having an opportunity denied, withdrawn or never available can and often does have the opposite debilitating effect.

Expectancy is about the mindset of the student prior to engaging with the experience. It's that moment where he or she is weighing up whether they are likely to be successful and, if so, how successful and at what cost. Researchers in this field talk up the importance of 'pre-decisional' and 'post-decisional' phases. By this they mean that students will use the pre-decisional phase to weigh up the value of a topic before committing effort to it. The post-decisional phase is about 'having got involved how do I now feel about it? Is it worth persisting with? Will it help me towards my goals?' If a student anticipates failure or a difficult emotional experience, motivation plummets. If, on the other hand, there are more positive associations, motivation goes up. How much it goes up depends upon the value assigned to the experience.

Value is about the perceived worth. How useful is this to me? The more direct benefit the student perceives, the more motivation skyrockets. Great teachers, like great leaders, sell benefits. To sell benefits you need to be certain about what they are and able to express them clearly. Do all your teachers know the benefits to learners of all the topics they teach? If teachers are convinced and very clear on benefits their motivation lifts and students pick up on this immediately. When teachers waffle on about having to do it because 'it's on the syllabus', watch as all motivation disappears like air from a punctured tyre.

Recommendation for teachers: sell the inherent value (benefits) to your students of engaging with learning.

In the project schools, the concept of student engagement was one with which all were concerned. I asked the question in each, 'How engaged are your students in their learning?' And at the same time attempted to find out whether 'engagement', however defined, was consistent across the school. One school defined engagement to include enquiring, listening and expressing; however, this seemed to operate within a narrow frame which was teacher initiated and directed. Listening attentively, recording notes, completing tasks, participating in discussion, showing consideration to others, being neat, checking work are all desirable learner behaviours but they can all coexist in a teacher directed, compliant environment where there is little or no choice.

The very wide range of responses within and across the schools showed how widely the notion of 'engagement' was interpreted.

- In all schools it included: paying attention, being on task, responding to questions, completing work

- In most it was the above plus asking good questions, taking time to think, seeing connections, helping others, being creative, offering ideas, asking for help

- In a few it was the above but also taking responsibility, being resilient, demonstrating skills, making informed choices.

All the project schools, and indeed every school I have visited recently, are challenged by a need to create more autonomous learners whilst at the same time retaining or exceeding academic performance. The concept of 'student voice' was a marker differentiating the core schools. Five schools showed a clear understanding and aspiration to embed this approach and had innovative practices in place. Five were aware of the challenge and thinking around it and five where it seemed counter to the ethos of the school.

Recommendation for teachers: aspire to a broad definition of what the student experience will be when they are 'engaged'. Ask what engagement means from the learner's point of view.

Keep your expectations high. There is a large amount of research that looks at the links between teacher expectation and student performance. In a pioneering 1968 study by Rosenthal and Jacobsen into the so-called 'Pygmalion effect' students were given an IQ test before 20 per cent were randomly selected and their teachers told that they had 'unusual potential for intellectual growth' and that they were expected to 'bloom' in academic performance throughout the year. At the end of the year, the students were administered the IQ test again and the results indicated a strong positive correlation between the teacher's expectations and the students' scores.

Things to do to ensure high teacher expectation:

- Talk up individual student success stories and treat these as precedents for what is to follow

- Have visible evidence of student success posted around the school

- Video students opening exam results in August, add uplifting music and show it to all staff on the first day of term

- Potential grades should always exceed predicted and work off ambitious potential grades

- Send student targets back if they are below Fischer Family Trust D

- Talk to your teachers through the communication you have with students. For example, in assemblies about performance and aspiration layer in messages for the teachers standing around the room about how they all expect so much of their students

- Have a whole school solution-focused approach to problem solving and train staff in its principles

- Challenge assumptions which are framed by negatives: can't, won't, unable, unwilling, lacking

- Ban pointless classroom activities! Start with a ban on colouring in, word searches, drawing posters, extended bouts of copying or dictation, finishing off or doing ten more for homework. Keep on learning through to the last day of each term.

Recommendation for teachers: **have high expectations – when you look at students do so in terms of their potential, not their past or their present performance – and prepare to be surprised.**

What is the impact of teachers favouring some groups of students over others? In class-rooms where teachers have a high differential in their treatment of students, where they favour brighter students and were noticed by the class members to be doing so, this influences achievement and students' expectations of themselves. The bigger the differential in how students are treated the more teacher expectation correlates with performance. When there is low differentiation, where everyone is treated alike, prior achievement is a better correlate to performance.

Teacher expectancy loops to and from student expectancy. Low teacher expectation of a group within a class is amplified when, at the same time, there is high expectation of others within the same class. Students pick up on what is being communicated, make comparisons and then begin to live up or down to those comparisons.

Things teachers should do to reduce differential expectation:

- Know all the names – and I mean all! This is the one thing that will make the most difference

- Laminate the names of all the students you teach on separate cards. Each card contains a photograph and any data or information you deem relevant to treating that person as an individual

- Use the cards to randomise questions, class roles or any other request made of students

- Download a random name generator, load the names of your classes and use it on the screen to 'select' volunteers

- Be open and honest with students about individual performance data

- Give small step feedback and teach them how to do the same for others in the class

- Teach the skills of self- and peer-evaluation

- Teach the skills of peer coaching

- Avoid unhelpful comparisons.

Recommendation for teachers: have a colleague observe your interactions with a range of classes noting who amongst the students gets your attention and what attracts that attention.

In the 1996 publication *Accelerated Learning in the Classroom*, I described how, as a consequence of miscommunication and a genuine error, a maths teacher who was new to a school had been misled into thinking she was teaching set two in maths for their GCSE when in fact it had been set four. Her expectations were so high the entire class outperformed all of those in set two, which was taught by someone else.

The set four teacher, Ani Magill, went on to become a highly successful head teacher and her school now epitomises the high expectations she was delivering in maths all those years ago. Her school, St John the Baptist, like all the other project schools, receives visitors from across the country keen to learn and adapt their practice. St John the Baptist makes a commitment to regularly get out and visit the best of what there is around the country. In more austere times this will be harder for most. But the benefits are enormous, especially so if you go with a clear focus and mob-handed! More than one of you and you can spread yourselves around, talk about what you saw on the way back and disseminate more effectively.

Here are some of the things she recommends you do in your school to raise expectations:

- Please don't decide what grades your class will get before you ever meet them. 'Set three only ever gets Ds etc.' Students are capable of great things if the teacher believes in them. I worked with a teacher in a secondary modern school whose mantra was '100 per cent can' (and they did).

- Catch the children being good, catch them being successful and let them know. In a school where a colleague was executive head for two terms, she sent a letter home to the parents of a Year 11 boy saying he was working well in design technology. His mother phoned to say it was the first nice letter she had received about her son in 12 years of education. From that point on, he stopped setting the fire alarm off!

- Grab the 'grey' children who work hard and go unnoticed – see them individually and tell them you are proud of them. It takes minutes and they feel ten feet tall.

- Tell your Years 10, 11, 12 and 13 they are the best year you've ever had and all the indications are that they will beat all previous records, even if they are a disaster!

Sometimes what is picked up on school visits are butterflies, small things which spread influence around. At Weydon School they have a staff member who is in charge of positivity and one of the things that has been introduced for students is the Weydon Bucket List – Ten Things You Will Do Before You Leave! Things on the bucket list include eating out in a restaurant with at least three other people, going to the dog racing and taking part in an overnight camping expedition.

Recommendation for teachers: do what you can to benefit from the best of what is around. A structured school visit that allows you to access alternative practice and benchmark your own can be better than any number of in-service events.

9. Fundamentals first

You can no longer get top grades by rote learning.

Head of Science, Haybridge School

Walthamstow School for Girls run a challenge called 'highdiving' for staff to try out new classroom ideas, new ways of learning and small innovations that would invigorate teaching. The best win the 'diving goggles' and retain them until another 'diver' proves their worth. Many schools start staff meetings with teaching and learning butterflies. Some ideas are so compelling they become viral. Fourteen years ago St John the Baptist School used accelerated learning ideas to identify ten features of a great lesson. This SJB Ten has been largely unchanged in that time. It appears in the school planner, the staff handbook, the head teacher's office, every classroom and on the website. It also appears in a slightly adapted form in lots and lots of other schools including four of our project schools.

This simple – but very powerful – idea is to work with staff to define what great learning looks and feels like. This is not what inspectors might say or a policy document recommend, it's a practical working tool from which staff can plan, observe, review and improve. Ideally it's done as a consequence of a practical and shared learning experience and not from discussion groups or working parties which tend to favour enthusiasts and the articulate. Some prior research may be needed to ensure that you don't recycle limited views and it will reward you to have the process planned in advance and facilitated.

At Weydon School continuing professional development is currently built around the question, 'What does great learning look like?' Equally the question could be, 'What makes an autonomous learner? Or 'What does independent learning look like?'

In *Blue Peter* style, here's one we did earlier, which is used to help structure our learning reviews.

Our ten fundamentals of great learning for staff:

1. Active engagement

2. Clarity of purpose

3. Use of assessment data to inform design

4. Organising and analysing information

5.   Problem solving

6.   Stretched through challenge

7.   Demonstrating understanding

8.   Progressing own learning

9.   Reviewing and evaluating

10. Personalisation and enjoyment.

The same but in a student friendlier format:

1.   Get involved and stay involved

2.   Be clear about what you are doing and what success will be like

3.   Know your targets and how to make progress towards them

4.   Collect, then organise, all the information you need

5.   Work towards positive solutions

6.   Try more difficult things to stretch yourself

7.   Explain your thinking as you go

8.   Check your progress regularly

9.   Review what you've learned

10. Plan how to use your new skills and knowledge.

At Chafford Hundred Campus they use their own classroom checklist. It features on all lesson plans, classroom observation sheets, learning walk profiles and in staff planners.

Once you have your own version, ensure that it is used to inform and enhance classroom practice across the whole school. The impact of having and embedding an agreed checklist of what constitutes great learning cannot be emphasised enough. It really will be the Trojan mouse that drives change forward. Eventually it will be so embedded into the thinking that it will no longer be seen as a 'requirement'.

Once you have your ten fundamentals of great learning in place then the school can use them creatively and for a variety of purposes in order to soak the strategies into the thinking of the school. Here are some suggested uses, others follow under the middle leader section on observation (page 139).

Classroom prompt: place a simple A2 poster at the front of the room so it acts as a prompt for both you and the class. The key to creating independent learners is that they know and understand the processes that underpin learning, so by making regular reference to the contents of the poster you help them understand the learning intentions that lie behind all of their classroom experiences.

Student prompt: place a student version in the back of the planner with an explanation that this is what your teachers think makes great learning. Set a home learning challenge to explain it to a parent, brother or sister and answer any questions they may have, then repeat the activity in pairs in class.

Recommendation for teachers: **use an agreed checklist of what constitutes great learning to help plan your lessons. Make sure all the elements are incorporated.**

In any learning environment you get more of what is reinforced. If you want more of any given behaviour in your classroom then capture that behaviour in the moment, describe it, promote it, celebrate it and then speculate with the student who exhibits the behaviour how he or she will transfer it. Having begun this, then ask others in your class to be doing the same when they see the behaviours.

If it takes 10,000 hours of directed practice to achieve mastery in any human discipline – playing the piano, chess, gymnastics, carpentry, surgery, snooker – it also requires some hours of practice to groove in the habits of great learning. Students don't come with this in place so be 100 per cent clear on the classroom learning protocols you wish to capture, describe, promote, celebrate and transfer.

In any classroom you want students to be able to ask great questions; listen to others; think things through; learn independently, in a pair, as part of a team and in a class. Here are some of the protocols used with younger learners to ensure this becomes the accepted behaviour in the class.

Questioning

Great questions
Do you:

- Take care over the question?

- Build on understanding?

- Make us think hard?

Listening

Great listening
Do you:

- Use your eyes and ears?

- Hear everything that's said?

- Think about what's said?

Thinking

Great thinking:
Do you:

- Take your time?

- Gather your thoughts?

- Think about the sequence of your thinking?

- Reach conclusions?

Solo learners

Great solos
Do you:

- Stay on task?

- Ask great questions?

- Gather information?

- Organise the information?

- Test the information?

- Reach your own conclusions?

Pair learners

Great pairs
Do you:

- Agree the question or task?

- Agree what's wanted?

- Help each other?

- Challenge each other?

- Review your progress?

Team learning

Great teams
Do you:

- Stay involved?

- Agree what's asked?

- Contribute?

- Check for progress?

- Complete what's asked?

Class learning

Great classes
Do you:

- Model respect?

- Keep your discipline?

- Listen when needed?

- Act when needed?

- Learn together?

These are the prompts I would use for KS3. No doubt you can adapt and improve them. They really have most power when used regularly by students as part of a strategy for them to self-monitor their engagement with learning processes. I'd recommend adding some design, using a program such as Flash so that they are interactive, then placing them on the school server so that every teacher has immediate access to them. Do the same on the student and parent portals.

Recommendation for teachers: define the classroom learning protocols you wish to promote. Display the protocols and reinforce them regularly.

10. Repertoire of strategies

It's more important to be a great teacher than a great specialist.

Teacher, Tudor Grange

Schools are improving in England yet, as the performance bar is raised, the gap between the best and the worst is not being narrowed. The gap between high performing schools and poorly performing schools in England remains marked. This is despite the number of secondary schools where less than 30 per cent of pupils gain five good GCSEs including English and maths, falling from 1,600 in 1997 to 247 in 2009 and where 100,000 more pupils achieve level four English and maths at the end of primary school each year.[12]

The gap between children from disadvantaged backgrounds and the rest is also considerable. At GCSE, 54.2 per cent of pupils not eligible for free school meals achieved five good GCSEs including English and maths, compared to 26.6 per cent of pupils known to be eligible for free school meals – an attainment gap of 27.6 percentage points. Working class boys eligible for free school meals do particularly badly. Only 19 per cent of white boys eligible for free school meals gain five good GCSEs and only 22.4 per cent of black Caribbean boys. Despite performance going up in all groups, a 'stubborn' gap remains. In 2006 the gap between white boys eligible for free school meals and all pupils was 33.9 percentage points. Three years later in 2009 it widened to 35.2 percentage points.[13]

So there are big gaps between schools and also between groups of students across and within schools. There are haves and have-nots. One of the worrying features is the within school variance in performance. Academics suggest there can be as much as 12 times more variation within a school than between schools. This means that some of the disadvantage can multiply up. Students with the best teachers in the best schools learn at least three times more each year than students with the worst teachers in the worst schools.[14] Therefore investing in the quality of teaching and teachers is a must.[15] To become a great teacher takes about eight years of full-time commitment but the teacher needs to develop through a combination of challenge, tacit and formal learning, being exposed to good practice and having space and opportunity to groove in good teaching habits.[16]

What you do on a daily basis as a teacher impacts directly on the life chances of the students in front of you. You can begin to compensate for some of the barriers described above. One of the most productive investments you and your school can make is in you!

Become a learner of the processes that shape learning – become a scientist investigating your own teaching.[17]

Recommendation for teachers: become more self-aware of what you do in the classroom and the impact it has on student learning: learn about your own teaching.

Do you teach history or do you teach GCSE history? Do you teach mathematics or do you teach A level mathematics? Do you teach your subject or how to pass exams in your subject? Are you a great specialist or a great teacher? If one or the other, how do you know? Why not both?

Great teachers have a repertoire of strategies that are based on an understanding of the process of learning. It's partly science and partly art. The science is in understanding the principles upon which learning is based and the art is in deploying those principles in different contexts. It's helpful to think of the repertoire of strategies as a continuum. The continuum extends from teacher directed learning at one end to student initiated learning at the other. Direct instruction to social constructivism; great teachers can move up and down the continuum as the circumstances demand.

Teacher roles

Some of the roles a teacher would adopt in moving along the continuum would be as follows:

- Instructor: directs students to essential information and rehearses the application of that information; stays focused on a narrow range of tasks
- Teacher: orchestrates the whole learning experience having chosen what is to be learned and how it will be learned
- Facilitator: structures learning situations which directly or indirectly extend the learning of the students; asks really good questions and works alongside the students as they search for solutions
- Coach: focuses on specific skills or techniques and works with the student to improve them
- Mentor: offers individual guidance to help maintain the students' capacity to deal with personal and interpersonal issues and to sustain personal resource
- Guide: provides general advice to help the student make informed choices

■ Role model: behaves in positive ways that will provide a template for the student to emulate.

The teacher would be able to assume several roles during one lesson, responding to the changing circumstances and demands of learning. In the very best practitioners the transitions would be smooth with roles overlapping, merging in and out of each other and the whole experience appearing seamless.

Recommendation for teachers: widen your repertoire of classroom intervention roles and practise moving between them.

There are social, emotional and cognitive dimensions to learning. Some youngsters, like some adults, prefer their own space and are happier learning on their own. Paired and small group learning are challenging contexts for these students. Others, more gregarious and extrovert perhaps, actively seek out peers with whom to engage in learning.

Our social dimensions to learning are therefore:

■ Individual

■ Pair

■ Group

■ Class

■ Community.

Learners perform better, stay involved longer and get more satisfaction and enjoyment from learning when they have efficacy within their preferred social dimension.[18] In other words, when students know how to go about learning on their own or in pairs, small groups or as a class they do better. As a teacher one cannot assume such skills are in place: you have to be very explicit in teaching them the associated skills. Academics call this meta-learning. Teach them to become meta-learners!

Should we have the equivalent of a pedagogy MOT in schools? It would be a fascinating exercise to concentrate on this alone. Is your class oriented to learning or performing? Classroom teachers experience a tension between getting youngsters through public examinations, the results of which shape their life chances, and equipping them to be better learners and so more able to cope with what life throws at them. In speaking to staff in the research schools about the student outcomes they desired, I asked the question, 'What do you wish your students to leave you and the school with?'

In each and every instance respondents linked personal skills and capabilities with academic outcomes suggesting that academic outcomes alone were insufficient preparation for life beyond school. One teacher at Seven Kings told me she felt she had a 'moral obligation' to engage students in her lessons. Another told me that his job was to help students 'understand geography and its processes, create global citizens and 21st century learners who can apply their learning skills in any context'. In Walthamstow a teacher with six years of experience responded that her job was to 'produce girls who embraced learning, would retain a passion for learning, pass exams and be able to do anything they wanted to do'. At Dixons I was told by two teachers with less than a year's experience each that it was to 'help students leave with a passion for learning, be proud of their achievements, do well and have choices and options as a consequence'. Across the schools the responses were similar; however the degree to which it went beyond an aspiration varied by school.

The ideal would be to have self-regulating, self-evaluating learners who were well motivated by learning and who continued to develop transferable learning skills and meta-cognitive strategies whilst achieving academically! What's more becoming nice people as they do so! This isn't happening as yet!

In *Learning, Performance and Improvement*, London-based academic Chris Watkins describes how the way teachers position tasks impacts significantly on pupil achievement: 'The most recent research shows that how the task is described – "to help you learn" versus "to see how good you are" – can influence a learner's orientation more strongly than the disposition that learners bring to the task.' Individual learners, groups and classes with a learning – as opposed to a performing – orientation do better. He goes on to cite further research, which shows 'that a class-average learning orientation has a positive effect on individual achievement gains, while class-average performance orientation has a negative effect'.

Recommendation for teachers: recalibrate the orientation in your classroom away from performing and more towards learning.

To begin to achieve the seeming impossible task of getting academic results whilst developing independent learning skills you will need to develop the capacity to transit from a performance-oriented teacher in a performance-oriented classroom to a learner-oriented teacher in a learner-oriented classroom. Many schools in our project are attempting to do this. It is not easy!

Performance-oriented classrooms	Transition	Learner-oriented classrooms
The teacher		**The teacher**
Instructs and directs		Teaches and guides
Emphasises answers		Emphasises questions
Has answers		Searches for answers
Selects content		Constructs options
Controls the pace		Orchestrates the pace
Asks the majority of questions		Encourages other's questions
Directs groupings		Invites groupings
Gives feedback based on completed outcomes		Gives feedback based on progress and next steps
Marks all contributions		Uses a variety of marking methods
Determines all assessment		Shares assessment criteria and techniques
Focuses on exams or tests		Focuses on incremental improvements

Performance-oriented classrooms	Transition	Learner-oriented classrooms
The learner		**The learner**
Follows instructions		Makes decisions
Must get it right		Must have a go
Wants the answer		Wants the method
Follows the teacher's logic and tries to get it right		Learns incrementally and by trial and error
Follows teacher's pace		Controls own pace
Answers teacher's questions		Answers own questions
Is grouped by the teacher		Elects who to learn with
Is rewarded upon completion		Is rewarded by effort
Is given a mark, level or grade		Understands and interprets their own mark, level or grade
Is assessed by the teacher		Is assessed by the teacher, themselves and peers
Focus is on becoming a better performer		Focus is on becoming a better learner
Is concerned with status and pecking order		Is concerned with progress and capacity to improve

There is good research to show the poor impact of teaching to the test.[19] Teachers, when pressured to teach to the test, favour the left-hand side of the tables above and adopt a 'transmission' model. This may be fine for some of the students but it will not help them become independent learners, nor will it benefit other students who prefer more 'active and creative' modes. The review by Harlen and Deakin Crick points out that 'students dislike high-stakes tests, show high levels of test anxiety (particularly girls) and prefer other forms of assessment'.[20]

Recommendation for teachers: use a structure based on learning to design all your lessons and extended learning experiences such as enquiry and project-based learning.

At Seven Kings I was told that a local authority inspector who had visited the school recently could not find one KS3 student who hadn't been interviewed about their learning in the previous three weeks.

One of the most powerful tools to help staff and students have a shared discussion about learning is an agreed architecture to lesson design. By designing a simple lesson structure based on an understanding of learning we create opportunities to improve the quality of discussion amongst staff across the school and with students in lessons. For schools that are a long way back on the learning journey this will be a great starting position. Here's the Accelerated Learning Cycle, which has been adapted and used by a number of the schools:

1. Connect

- Use a short, engaging starter activity that is relevant

- Discuss what they already know or want to know about the topic

- Build on their thoughts

- Be positive in what you do, what you say and how you say it

- Connect it all up: what's gone before and what's to come.

2. Outcomes

- Share content, process and benefits

  - Content -what we will learn

  - Process – how we will learn

  - Benefits – why it's worth learning

- Differentiate the above – use the taxonomies described below to help.

3. Activate

- Turn the information to be learned into a problem to be solved

- Make the learning engaging by structuring variety and progressive challenge into tasks

- Provide any resources and discuss sources of information

- If required, encourage them into appropriate learning units – pairs, groups, teams

- Be deliberate in drawing attention to learning processes throughout the lesson

- Stay positive.

4. Demonstrate

- Allow them to present their solutions. Provide time to redraft or tweak their solutions based on feedback

- Get them into pairs or groups so that they can help each other improve on their solutions. Give feedback and encourage them to reflect on the feedback and, in turn, give feedback to others

- Invite really good questions and build a climate of evaluation

- Reinforce the learning behaviours you wish to promote.

5. Consolidate

- Review content, process and benefits

- Ask them to explain which learning skills they have developed

- Talk with them about how they can use what they learned in other lessons

- Preview what's coming next.

Once an architecture is in place for lesson design, then the language – connect, outcomes, activate, demonstrate, consolidate or their equivalents – becomes everyday parlance within the school. In one of the schools students have been heard to 'assist' supply teachers by reminding them of the stages of learning.

Cramlington, Sandringham, Seven Kings, St John the Baptist and Chafford are amongst a number of schools which deliberately share a vocabulary for learning. Researchers estimate that, between starting school and finishing in the sixth form, students come across 85,000 different words in print.[21] Some of these words will be taught formally; most will be encountered in context. It is said that it takes at least six encounters before an able student begins to make connections and can use a word in context for themselves. Students have planners with vocabulary lists by subjects in most schools but very few have learning vocabularies.

As an example of what's possible, here's a vocabulary list we recommend at my company Alite for helping to support thinking skills.

Bronze thinking words

balance, category, classify, compare, contrast, decision, different, evidence, fact, fairness, judge, know, memory, opinion, reason, similar, solution, sort, test, value

Silver thinking words

abstract, assumption, belief, bias, claim, consequence, contradict, credibility, criteria, estimate, evaluate, explanation, interrogate, locate, logic, speculation, theory, trial, understand, valid

Gold thinking words

condition, conjecture, corroborate, data, distort, empathise, exaggerate, fallacy, hypothesis, implication, inductive, infer, innovate, interrogate, norm, presume, supposition, synthesis, system, viewpoint

Taught out of context, this list would be of limited use. Built up in lessons and through regular use, this wider vocabulary ramps up the quality of discussion around learning and takes it to a higher order. Students with more elaborated conceptions of learning perform better in public exams and, according to Watkins and others, lower attainment at that age is correlated with perceived pressure from adults while higher attainment is positively related to independence, competence and a meaning-oriented approach to learning.[22]

One final point about vocabulary: one school has it woven into the fabric of the building. At Cramlington Learning Village, the five Rs – resilience, resourcefulness, responsibility, reasoning and reflection – are built into the glass and brick structures of their new Junior Learning Village; in the older part of the school the assembly hall curtains have the five Rs woven in!

Recommendation for teachers: **have learning conversations with your students. Build a vocabulary of learning. Focus discussion principally on the processes of learning, not on passing tests or question spotting for exams.**

Better use of visual reinforcement in schools is something that is not given the attention it deserves. It can be a short cut to influencing teacher behaviours and reinforcing some consistency of response across the school.

Some schools and some trusts, particularly those with new builds, are taking the decision to go for a supermarket or art gallery look with pristine, white walls and visual display confined to the television screens around the school and the electronic whiteboards in classrooms. They argue that a 'corporate' feel with a sophisticated visual environment makes students feel more adult and so are more likely to be enervated by the look and feel of what's around them and more respectful of the site as a whole. In some respects this is a kick against the proliferation of scruffy hand-written posters that can festoon corridors and make them appear like the small ads in the newsagent's window. I think the best solutions lie somewhere in-between.

Humans are phenomenally well adapted for remembering the look of things, particularly faces, places and spaces. One bland surface, whether it be a corridor wall, a page in a textbook or a badly designed worksheet, is much like any other. By designating spaces that contain visual information useful to support learning we can keep the integrity of the look whilst exploiting the opportunity for locating distinctive visual cues. Many classroom teachers make time-consuming mistakes regarding the use of visual display. Here are the most common:

- Visual information which cannot be seen easily, read or understood

- Explanations of levels written in gobbledygook

- Fonts and visuals which are too small, too confusing or outdated

- Display that does not support learning in any way and is never referred to or made use of

- Display that is perfect student work or exemplar work – often put up to incentivise, it most often has the opposite effect

- Too much material, so it becomes overwhelming

- Students work mounted and displayed to recognise effort – again often demotivational

- Mass-produced posters with cheesy messages that do not have any connection with the students in the room.

There are five really good ways to use visual reinforcers. If your school has a corporate approach to the seen environment then these reinforcers appear in the proscribed way and in the designated spots, otherwise apply them in your own classroom.

- Protocols for learning – easily seen, easy to read and simple guidelines to reinforce learning behaviours

- Tools for learning – tools that can be used to support questioning or higher order thinking

- Attitudes to learning – affidavits from known personalities or past students with motivational messages

- Approaches to learning – as opposed to exemplar and perfection, drafts, redrafts and final versions with students' own and peer comments attached (see below)

- Cool stuff to talk about – topical quotes, images, items that can be used to trigger discussion with students.

Following some development work in a school I had an email exchange with some colleagues where we attempted to agree a rationale for a different approach to visual learning. Here's the final summary.

As you say there is a lot in this.

Clearly it's important to be consistent in the messages given out and my message was about positivity and more significantly about reinforcing the learning and the learning behaviour you want more of. There is an unquestioning acceptance that displaying children's work is a good thing. Local authorities run courses on it. In 20 years of visiting schools and researching I've seen no evidence from academics, children or staff that mounting completed work enhances children's learning or their esteem: none whatsoever. In many cases it does the opposite. That said, this does not mean we should not use display but when we do so we should use it wisely as the hours involved can be onerous.

There are three levels I recommend: learning protocols such as good asking etc.; learning tools such as thinking skills, great questions to ask, essential vocabulary; finally motivational guidance – how to do well in languages, why languages are important etc. Then there is the display relating to the learning process. This tends to be good in D&T where process is important but absent elsewhere. This is where you can make a difference.

When it's done best it can show the development of work from early drafts to final product reinforcing the point that perfection is not a given; it can be annotated by other students to capture the best elements of the learning process or what's admired by peers; it can be a portfolio of contributions in a variety of formats around a topic or theme; it can be guidance from students about how to complete a task or topic; it can be the outcomes of student or staff surveys on what they like about the subject; it can be what public figures say about learning or the subject.

The possibilities to reinforce learning and learning behaviours are endless and display is a key part of it. In every presentation (now hundreds) I've ever given to primary schools I've warned them of the inherent dangers of a 'good work board' mindset and the endless hours they put into classroom display – and I mean hours and hours – most of which are about making the room look brighter. I'm 100% against the 'good work board' approach as it rewards all the wrong things. If it's not about learning or contributing directly to children's learning then I ask primary colleagues to be very clear that the hours spent 'double mounting' are worth it. The primary school head I spoke to yesterday has used Accelerated Learning (AL) for years in his own school and in the school they took out of special measures. He was very clear on what it had done for his own career and for the schools where he had been Head Teacher (HT). My approach to display in primary schools is quite radical but has always been consistent: too many so-called experts are telling teachers to spend hours on display, using up valuable time for questionable outcomes. If teachers are questioning it then that's a very good thing!

Properly done it brings the class together around learning and the process of learning so for that reason I think your criteria for selection in MFL is more of a barrier to most students than an invitation. Not all will be able to show great use of the language but many will want to; not all, especially boys, will present their drawings well; accuracy is desirable yes, but so is taking a risk and giving it your best shot whatever; being an example to others is fine but it's the next step that's important for most learners not the finished perfect product. I think your criteria will make languages more formidable for most students.

It's a personal point of view on my part about display and not a view on any one department. I hope this explains my thinking, why it's important and that it gives you and the school some points to act on.

Best wishes

Alistair

Cramlington Learning Village has an electronic learning wall in every classroom via the school server. It contains their five Rs with student-friendly explanations of each against levels, tools such as De Bono's thinking hats or Andersen's revised thinking taxonomy, traffic lights and a range of simple thinking tools. St John the Baptist has an electronic wall with the addition of starter tools: images, music, countdown clock.

The 'destinations wall' was seen again and again, prominently and proudly positioned in schools. It had particular power where quotes were placed alongside the photographs and where the photographs were taken at or around the destination. It's considerably more motivational to see someone whom you recognise standing in a hard hat on an oil rig a year on from leaving school or outside a student halls of residence with their friends or singing in a university chapel than in their school uniform looking awkward!

Recommendation for teachers: use visuals to identify, reinforce and improve learning behaviours.

11. Stretched through challenge

If you want to go beyond outstanding you have to let people work it out.

Stephen Munday, Head Teacher, Comberton

One of the difficulties you face teaching within tight time units is the limited opportunities for students to practise their learning skills. Several of the project schools use im-aginative interventions to get round this problem. In doing so they have used four different strategies:

- parallel pedagogies

- stretched timings

- rich tasks

- real audiences and outcomes.

Some staff at Cramlington Learning Village design extending tasks using SOLO (Structure of the Observed Learning Outcome). SOLO provides a 'systematic way of describing how a learner's performance grows in complexity when mastering many tasks, particularly the sort of tasks undertaken in school'. It's a way of designing tasks so that they are progressively more demanding and also assessing the outcomes at each level. At the first or *pre-structural* level students haven't really understood the point and approach the task naively. At the next or *uni-structural* level one aspect of the task is focused on stepping up to the next *multi-structural* level. Beyond that several aspects of the task are picked up and used, but are treated independently and additively. As we progress to higher levels of sophistication the student approach becomes more *relational* with different aspects of the tasks integrated into a coherent whole and then what's called *extended abstract* where the previous integrated whole may be conceptualised at a higher level of abstraction and generalised to a new topic or area.

Another method used to support the design of extended tasks and challenges by staff at Cramlington Learning Village is TASC (Thinking Actively in a Social Context). TASC is a thinking skills approach used by students. Organised in an easy-to-follow, eight-step structure, the wheel is a really good tool for helping a learner approach a research or enquiry-based task.

Learning Futures promote two methods that have emerged from some of the schools with which they work. Enquiry-based learning (EBL): seeking out and evaluating information in order to answer open-ended questions and solve open-ended problems. Project-based learning (PBL): carrying out an extended project that produces a tangible output. Learning Futures suggests these two methods are enhanced by being combined: 'Enquiry is most powerful when it is part of a project with tangible results, while students learn most from projects that are propelled by open (but scaffolded) enquiry.'

Project-based learning at Seven Kings takes the form of a one-week profound question challenge. Students from vertical tutor groups – Years 7, 8, 9, 10 and 12 – work for a week in groups of 16 to create their own profound question, construct their own assessment rubric and formulate their own desired outcomes. Smaller sub-groups, which are mixed ability and mixed age, then supervise themselves in pursuit of answers to their question.

At Sandringham in the last month of Year 7 no homework is set; instead they have a project fair – an idea from 'Engaging Minds' – where all departments create a project, students choose one, and work in groups for homework. It is then presented to parents at school and has no teacher input. This promotes independent learning and releases time for staff to write reports at this time of year. Students from Years 8 and 9 mentor the younger students as they have participated in this sort of learning and teamwork before.

Dixons Academy uses a Year 9 independent learning project which comprises 15 lessons around a research topic – such as 'Who do we think we are?' – before students present their findings in a series of presentations.

Cramlington Learning Village decided to replace activities week with personal challenge week. The difference is important. Activities week is often about staff putting on things that reflect their own interests, with a best guess at what some of the students would like and a feel for what would be good for them. Many schools, of which Cramlington is one, have turned this on its head.

Students are surveyed as to what personal challenge they think they would like to undertake. What then happens is that students opt in, negotiate and agree groups for their chosen activity where they are needed and are then briefed on the challenge. They can change their mind after the briefing but only once. They are advised that over the course of the five-day experience they will be expected to show evidence of significant learning and that a debriefing looking at the attributes they have needed will take place each day. This is Monday to Friday. On the Saturday morning each group shows their learning in a public performance which takes place at the school. The parents and members of the community of the town of Cramlington are invited.

Recommendation for teachers: provide opportunities for learners to demonstrate their independent learning skills. Such opportunities necessitate longer time frames, mixed groups, open-ended tasks with genuine outcomes.

After-school clubs, revision and top-up classes and sessions for parents on how to help your child succeed occur across most of our schools. At St Bonaventure's School there are Saturday morning clubs in English, maths and science. The clubs are voluntary with students signing up for them in advance each Monday. Teachers take turns on a rota to lead the clubs. It's all done on a voluntary basis with no additional payments. There are two-, one- and- a half-hour sessions and 150 students attend! Here are some other ideas for improving exam performance:

- Put revision materials on iPods, MP3 players, etc. so that students can access their revision at their convenience.

- If you use electronic resources (PowerPoints etc.) then make these available online or on a CD.

- Invest in digital voice recorders to allow staff to record 'top ten tips' from this lesson and upload to the school learning platform. Some of these recorders have a USB stick built in so no leads are required and the resulting podcast can be uploaded with no stress. Students can download and listen to this as needed. Every bit helps and students are more likely to use this than their exercise books.

- Have subject-specific resources for parents. Limit the amount of information to the equivalent of one side of A4 per subject. Call them Ten Steps to Success in … Introduce it via a parental support evening led by subject leaders and students and then put it up on the school website.

- Don't run open revision classes because the wrong students come. Target which students are to attend. Write home and explain why it is essential they come.

- Plan individual revision timetables for students to come into school during the exams. Some won't need it but most won't do any effective revision without your help. Co-ordinate this centrally. Send the revision timetables to parents and phone home every time someone misses one.

- Publish past papers, mark schemes and examiners' reports on the departmental web page or on the school intranet so that students can see just what makes the difference between an A*/A/B and C/D.

- Have a departmental revision evening that is open to all students a couple of days before the examination. Plan it so that each member of the department is present. Arrange for pizza and sweets at the end of the session (don't tell students it will be at the end). Target groups so that students on G grades are not paired with A*/A grade students as this might cause demotivation and self-doubt.

- Provide breakfast on exam days and ensure students have a bottle of water in the exam.

- Encourage everyone in the department to talk to all the students as they walk into the exam – smile and wish them luck!

- Be available before the start of each exam to give some final tips. This is perfectly acceptable so long as you have not looked at the paper and the exam officer knows. Remember everyone at school has the same goal in sight – students achieving the highest possible grades.

- When students come out of exam paper one, give them a letter with information on what they need to do for paper two. If possible, provide a question and model answers. Remind them they are nearly there!

- Never allow a student to resit a module without additional revision input. Have a system in place otherwise it will push stress elsewhere and the student won't achieve higher anyway!

- Make mock examinations as realistic as possible – students to sit in the same rooms, with the same rules and routines. Don't just give last year's paper. Try to work out routines for what is most likely to come up.

- Provide mock exam results on a 'results day' in a brown envelope to raise their status. All students will be able to collect their results at the same time. This raises the status and importance of exams.

- Don't let your Year 11 students drop subjects in order to 'to concentrate on their other subjects'. This is a euphemism for wandering the corridors. If a student is likely to achieve more by reducing their entries have a very tight programme either with a mentor, teaching assistant, one-to-ones with really good teachers or a member of the school leadership team. Use this time to get all the homework and any coursework done so nothing has to be done at home.

Lots of effort goes into exam preparation. As a general rule, 'spaced rehearsal' – a little and often – is better for learning so don't leave it late to get students ready. One-off events such as study skills or super learning days have minimal impact especially if they are not integrated into a bigger programme or followed up.

Recommendation for teachers: think strategically in preparing students for exams. Consider the social, emotional, physiological and cognitive dimensions to performance. It's not about cramming!

I taught a group of adult prisoners in a prison in the north-west of England for a two-hour session on life skills. It was 1984. The door was locked and you signed for the resources, in this case a felt pen and five sheets of flip-chart paper. That would be that for the next two hours. No plugs, no batteries! What would be the minimum classroom resource you would expect to have now to teach your students in school? Would you require objects with plugs or batteries? Could you get by without? For how long could you get by without?

If you don't do social networks, don't tweet or Skype, can't decide if you are a technophobe or technocrat, digital migrant or digital native then you are probably a baby boomer and ready for some guidance on basic e-learning. A blog[23] about the World Innovation Summit for Education (WISE) conference in Doha December 2010 had the author suggest:

> We get 'talked at' in schools, 'lectured' to in HE, suffer the stupid 'breakout group' method in training and spend far too much of our lives in useless, often unnecessary 'meetings'. This was the baby boomers' approach to collaboration and sharing. Compare this to the immediacy of mobile, texting, messaging, posting, commenting, tweeting, social networking, blogging, team-based gaming, skyping, filesharing and crowdsourcing. We have more to learn from them, than them from us.

We have more to learn from them, than them from us! One of the pieces of technology that will become increasingly redundant over the next few years is the electronic whiteboard.[24] They will gradually disappear as schools realise they are too inflexible and tie the teacher to the front. They will be replaced by an older technology known as a 'wall'. Adaptability, mobility and immediacy will be increasingly important and we will see a mixed economy of technologies. At Dixons Academy they have a well-established media and ICT infrastructure that utilises:

- the teaching resource eStream which is searchable

- discussion forums

- student blogs

- wikis

- voting pads

- Flip Video cameras

- podcasting

- interactive tags – QR (Quick Response) codes

- multi-media recording studio and video unit.

The innovative UK-based, assessment software company Smartassess have already created a technology that will allow all the students in a school to have a personalised single log-in to help them access free Web 2.0 tools such as Google Docs. Thinking in the future will move from seeing school ICT as a content-delivery mechanism with schools spending large amounts of money installing and maintaining a virtual learning environment, to the world of 'apps', which allow you to create great content. Share it, collaborate on it and evaluate it through feedback.

Recommendation for teachers: **use technology in service of learning and to attain your learning outcomes, not for its own sake or because it's inherently engaging.**

Different stages of learning provide opportunities for the use of simple software applications and Web 2.0 tools. Web 2.0 tools are those that support collaboration, and are interactive and promote sharing: social network sites, blogs, wikis, RSS (Really Simple Syndication), photograph and video sharing being examples.

Questions should precede your use of a tool. Is it the simplest technology to deliver the outcomes you seek? Does it support your learning intentions? Does it add a dimension for a student that is both necessary and unique? Is it time efficient? Is it accessible to all? Can student progress be recorded? Are students aware of the learning processes they are going through as they use the tool? Once you have answered these questions then your choice of tools should emerge from pedagogy rather than availability or novelty. For example, here are some examples of tools that support different phases of learning.

Initiating thinking and for starter activities

- Wordle. Students scan in text, and Wordle highlights and re-emphasises the most used words. Wordle was used to summarise text in this book.

Wallwisher. A noticeboard for posting notes, comments and peer feedback.

Boggle. A simple and engaging word game.

Timers. Online clocks which count up or down.

Communicating learning outcomes

YouTube. Either your own videos uploaded or those relating to the topic.

CrazyTalk. Animate any image or photograph of a face. Choose a famous personality or historical figure. Allow the character to introduce the outcomes.

Glogster. Online posters.

Activating engagement

PhotoPeach. A slide show with a twist! Add quizzes and commentaries.

Prezi. An improvement on PowerPoint that allows more real, authentic navigation.

DoInk. Students can create their own animations.

TED. Some brilliant, short talks by some of the greatest thinkers in the world.

Wikis. A wiki would allow a group of students to build a knowledge bank related to a subject or to a class topic. Any student with a password can go in, edit, write and save.

Blogs. Students can write their own or contribute to the class or subject blog.

Sharing and collaborating on tasks

Google Docs. Collaborate on projects in real time. Students can work together on any shared document. Documents could be newsletters, articles, plans, drawings or spreadsheets.

Stixy. Users create tasks, appointments, files, photos, notes and bookmarks on their Stixyboards.

CoveritLive. Track and record a learning experience online. Add files, images, sound, commentary and share in a community.

Storybird. Collaborative storytelling.

Reviewing

- SurveyMonkey. Online questionnaire.
- Flip Video. Brilliant piece of kit that allows you to film in high resolution with good sound and then to show it immediately through a USB which flips open.
- Quizlet. Create your own quizzes and review games.
- Lino. Like electronic Post-it notes – great for peer review.

Recommendation for teachers: become acquainted with the basic classroom technologies and also have working familiarity with technologies which extend beyond the classroom.

One of the recent innovations, which has added an extra dimension to the professional development of teachers, is micro-blogging. Micro-blogging consists of very short messages sent out – usually with links to attached files – to the users within the network. The best-known example is Twitter. Most non-users know of Twitter through celebrity 'tweeters'.[25] In fact what lies within Twitter, for those who care to look, are tightly integrated networks of educationalists who support each other in sharing blogs, audio and video files and presentations. What this provides is a constant stream of up-to-the-minute information from sources of your choosing. Teacher tweeters tell me that they delete the bores that only ever tweet about their daily routines in favour of professionals who link in to the best of what's going on. By the use of hash tags it's possible to narrow the information to topics of your own choosing. It has phenomenal potential for teachers and for schools.

As a consequence of social networking and the micro-blogging phenomenon, informal communities of teachers organise themselves to share technology. TeachMeet events take place all over the UK and beyond. They are self-organising activities with very short multi-media inputs on topics of shared interest. There are micro-presentations – lasting seven minutes, and nano-presentations – lasting two minutes at most with up to five in quick succession. There will be a multi-media recording or recordings of the event with opportunities for those who are not physically present to participate. Staff travel a long way to take part and do so voluntarily. There are no gurus, few egos and no platforms. Promoted virally, TeachMeet attracts the staff from schools who are exceptionally well informed about Web 2.0 and its potential to support learning.

Some of the staff I spoke to from Cramlington Learning Village also talked of being part of the Microsoft Partners in Learning network.

Recommendation for teachers: obtain a Twitter account and follow some of the leading educationalists and edu-technologists who post there. Attend TeachMeet events in your area.

From the experience of meeting enthusiasts for Web 2.0 tools it becomes immediately apparent that they are often isolated within their schools. Some are self-confessed geeks who because of their knowledge and interest prefer to hold electronic conversations and share their work collaboratively than talk about it to many of their colleagues in their own schools.

There are a number of challenges here. The first is to utilise the knowledge that sits within our midst. The second is to protect the investment of time and resource. Time spent on engaging with new technologies, Web 2.0 tools and software applications has to be time well spent. Ensuring that we know and understand the principles of great learning and are able to apply those principles has to be the determining factor in how students interface with the electronic media in the school environment.

12. Beyond outstanding

Do you know what an outstanding lesson looks like? If we have already identified what great learning looks like then translating it into a primer for lessons is relatively straight-forward. There are different ways of defining what an outstanding lesson might look like; one is to start with observable features.

Here are our ten observable features of outstanding lessons:

1. **Active engagement**

    - Choice
    - Decision making
    - Responsibility.

'Students demonstrate excellent concentration and are rarely off task even in extended periods without direction from an adult.'

They are involved in making choices and decisions over how they learn and assume responsibility for their own learning and the learning of others.

2. **Clarity of purpose**

    - Knowing what
    - Knowing how
    - Knowing why.

'Students know and understand what they are learning, how they will be learning and why they are learning.'

They know and understand the subject content, the process of how they will be learning and the benefits to them of the learning both inside and outside school.

3. **Use of assessment data**

    - Planning
    - Feedback
    - Differentiation.

'Students are given tasks that have been planned carefully to meet their learning needs based on assessment data.'

They have the opportunity whilst learning to get and give feedback. Tasks are adapted for individuals and groups based on this feedback.

4. **Organising and analysing information**

    - Identification
    - Investigation
    - Explanation.

'Students are able to find and analyse a range of information from a variety of sources.'

With the information they have found, they are able to identify patterns and trends as well as organise the results into a coherent explanation of the problem or issue being studied.

5. **Problem solving**

    - Focused on solutions
    - Strategies and tools
    - Questioning and creativity.

'Students are focused on the big picture and come up with solutions to problems rather than be focused on limited tasks.'

They are aware of, and persist with, a range of appropriate thinking strategies and tools to solve problems. They are encouraged to ask rich questions and be creative.

6. **Stretched through challenge**

    - Positive attitude
    - Resilience
    - Extending tasks.

'Students are prepared to tackle challenging tasks and issues with a positive attitude and are resilient.'

Learning tasks are predominantly 'low threshold, high ceiling' allowing all to be challenged.

7. **Demonstrating understanding**

- Variety of methods
- Application
- Grasp.

'Students are given the opportunity to demonstrate their understanding through a variety of methods.'

Their demonstrations show clear application to the problem being studied and real grasp of the core ideas.

8. **Progressing own learning**

- Commitment
- Self-assessment
- Improvement strategies.

'Students' keenness and commitment to succeed and ability to grasp opportunities to extend and improve their own learning is exceptional.'

They are aware of where they are in terms of teacher and self-assessment and what strategies they can use to improve. Progress is at least good for some groups and is exemplary for others.

9. **Reviewing and evaluating**

- Focused on learning outcomes
- Ongoing in lesson
- Teacher-, peer- and self-assessment.

'Students have the opportunity, in a variety of ways, to review and evaluate against learning outcomes at appropriate times during the lesson.'

There is a culture of evaluation in the class where self- and peer-assessment is encouraged and improvement and progress is championed.

10. **Personalisation and enjoyment**

- Individualised
- Adapted

● Absorbed and enthused.

Learning is well adapted to, and shows an excellent understanding of, individual need. Students obviously enjoy their learning and show real enthusiasm in the lesson. They are absorbed with the learning tasks, want to know more and transfer what's learned beyond the classroom.

At Tudor Grange staff say that Years 7, 8 and 9 are noticeably more independent in their approach to learning and how they conduct themselves around the school. This is attributed to a large degree to their Skills Action Service Programme (SASP) which the school designed as a means of building confidence and communication skills in young learners.[26] Much of what takes place is outside of any classroom and takes the younger students to the edge of their comfort zone.

Seven Kings staff also notice a positive difference between the attitude to learning of their younger students in Years 7 and 8 compared with Year 12. The younger children ask better questions, assume responsibility for learning quicker, don't wait for help or to be told what to do and are better than their elders at paired and group learning. This, they claim, is entirely down to the younger students being taught the skills of learning. One of the outcomes sought for students at Seven Kings is that they can learn the skills in one context and transfer those skills into another.

At Seven Kings students:

lead starters in the connection phase of learning

lead plenaries either when asked to do so or when they think it appropriate

lead group sessions

attend departmental meetings

from Year 10 upwards observe teachers and give feedback using criteria based on qualified teacher status

who are subject *experts* wear high visibility vests.

At Sandringham they have developed the learning skills of students so successfully that they can model great learning behaviours: asking higher order questions, facilitating groups, running plenary sessions. Two students from each tutor group were trained by a member of the SLT to run plenaries.

The students then tried them in ten lessons and kept a logbook of their experiences, as well as an online discussion forum. They then did a 'big switch' where they did it in other lessons in which they had not taken part. Staff also did a 'big switch' and allowed students to run question-and-answer sessions and reviews in other lessons, thus modelling and so making significant the skill of asking the right questions to reinforce learning.

One development at Sandringham is to encourage parents to mark students' books by constructing a parent-friendly assessment pro forma.

I think it is very difficult to go beyond outstanding when you are teaching in 45-, 50- or 55-minute periods. At Haybridge and Cramlington Learning Village the learning sessions are 75 minutes and 150 minutes. This allows for extended learning to occur.

The 'lead lesson' concept with larger mixed groups, having intensive high quality priming inputs from the best teachers before moving into smaller groups who then pursue a set of related questions or a set of tasks, was being trialled at Tudor Grange when I visited. The classroom spaces were being opened up to accommodate up to 90 students. High quality presentation equipment with a large screen is placed towards the front, with smaller screens around the room and round tables towards the back for more informal co-operative learning.

At Tudor Grange they are developing the concept of the lead lesson. In the humanities department at Cramlington Learning Village, classes are merged so that two teachers with support staff teach up to 60 students. Teachers plan together (often across disciplines), and this adds further flexibility to the timetable. Staff at Cramlington Learning Village are in demand from Building Schools for the Future programme schools around the country to go and speak to them about project-based and enquiry-based learning and the use of large teaching spaces.

If you consider our criteria for learning that is beyond Ofsted's outstanding you can see that the significant difference is in learner autonomy and decision making.

Here are our ten observable features of 'beyond outstanding' lessons:

1. **Proactive engagement**
   Students are involved in all phases of the experience, actively participating in choices over purpose, content, scope and methods of learning.

2. **Clarity of purpose**
   Students are clear about what, how and why they are learning and exhibit significant autonomy in how they will apply their learning.

3. **Ownership of the assessment process**
   Students develop and negotiate success criteria and the related assessment tasks and initiate self-, peer- and group- assessment.

4. **Organise, analyse and utilise relevant information**

    Students locate, organise and analyse information from a range of sources, and then synthesise that information to progress learning tasks. In doing so they use thinking tools and new technology imaginatively.

5. **Direct enquiry and independent problem solving**

    Students define problems and work collaboratively and methodically to generate solutions at all phases of the learning process. They exhibit skills, practical problem solving strategies and use of relevant technologies.

6. **Stay actively involved at all stages of complex learning challenges**

    Students exhibit a 'growth mindset' showing self-awareness of themselves as learners, whilst remaining positive and engaged throughout.

7. **Demonstrate their own learning and understanding**

    Students elect to exhibit their learning and understanding using a variety of methods, opportunities and locations. In doing so they show depth of understanding and fluency in thinking.

8. **Measure and direct their own progress**

    Students are skilled at calibrating levels of progress and building self-evaluation into a repertoire of improvement techniques. They are making decisions on how to progress.

9. **Habitually review and evaluate for improvement**

    Students seek opportunities, in a variety of ways, to review and evaluate against their outcomes at appropriate times during learning.

10. **Meaningful to the individual**

    Students show an enjoyment for learning and for autonomous enquiry. Learning is transferred and prolonged beyond the institution and so provides a sense of agency.

Recommendation for teachers: **think beyond outstanding. Inspection criteria cannot be ignored but shouldn't become a brake on what's possible.**

Three:
The human pyramid – managers supporting

Human pyramids can be dangerous. With every level you add the less stable it becomes.

Ric Wallenda, base of the seven-man high wire pyramid, The Flying Wallendas

Middle leader talk

The words and phrases most used by middle leaders in our interviews:

Challenge and Support

13. The middle leader role

The results stop with the learning leader and here the momentum takes you, you can't let the students or the team down.

Middle Leader, Seven Kings

Are you first and foremost a subject leader, head of department, middle manager or middle leader? How would you describe yourself? Which term would you prefer?

In the individuals and teams I interviewed there was a difference in how some middle leaders saw their role and how school leadership saw it. All middle leaders were able to talk about the 'team' and used expressions such as support, development, commitment and sharing more readily and more easily than terms like challenge, accountability, monitoring and responsibility. The flow of the conversations and the comments I recorded left me with a strong impression that many, maybe most, saw themselves as defenders of subject and department, then leaders and developers of the team, and were slow to talk up any monitoring function. In schools that were more vertically structured this seemed more so. Middle leaders are in the Janus-faced role of being accountable to their line management whilst, at the same time, line managing others. They are expected to support but also to challenge. It seems the former sits more easily.

The research literature suggests that the primacy of subject knowledge and subject teaching in the professional identity of middle leaders – how they are recruited and how they are perceived by colleagues – plays a part in inhibiting them from becoming involved in wider school roles. It is also apparent that the more the middle leader is encouraged to be 'one of us' the more problematic the monitoring of colleagues becomes. Often they position themselves or have become positioned as lead practitioners and managers of the 'student offer' rather than managers of their colleagues. What appears to be a collegiate management with shared decision making is often rhetoric, more 'aspired to than real' and a mask for departmental autonomy. Sitting within that autonomy can be an unwillingness to hold others to account. The real challenge and the most demanding aspect of the job is for middle leaders to balance this natural tendency to favour the 'nice' parts of the job with challenge, the 'not so nice' part!

Recommendation for middle leaders: write down your preferred role descriptor or words which best describe your role. Ask your 'team' to do the same for you. What terms are used?

School structure can provide either a boost or a barrier to whole school change. In the schools that had a strong departmental structure, in some instances with as many staff as a small school, there was significantly less evidence of engagement with whole school approaches to learning and teaching. These were semi-autonomous fiefdoms. In such instances I saw more conservatism around learning and teaching, more preoccupation with the integrity of the subject and fewer imaginative approaches to staff development. I asked all middle leaders and young teachers whether it was more important to be a good subject specialist or to be a good teacher. In the schools with a strong departmental structure the young teachers particularly talked up the importance of subject expertise with middle leaders cool on the idea that a good teacher could deliver without any subject background.

Where school leadership teams had promoted collegiate decision making around the implementation of whole school issues such as, for example, assessment for learning or coaching, there was more evidence of middle leaders interacting with each other and sharing good practice. This multiplied the opportunities for informal discussion on learning and teaching issues and paved the way for the sharing of good practice, particularly in classroom observation.

At Walthamstow School for Girls each faculty has an ICT representative, a special educational needs representative and a gifted and talented representative. These cross-school teams meet half-termly. At Dixons middle leaders have 'a strong sense of autonomy' and are seen as the sounding board for ideas. Middle leaders participate in a school improvement group (SIG) with a remit to work on cross-academy improvements. Participants apply for the opportunity, are interviewed and if successful are paid a stipend. Within the group they pair with another colleague to pursue school-based research. The diverse composition of the SIG ensures that 'everybody buys into our learning and teaching recommendations, subject by subject – there's never any of this maths is different attitude!' In interviewing the leadership team they commented on the importance of doing things together: 'Our staff don't take risks so we need to train and retrain and do things together.'

Recommendation for middle leaders: **identify how you might find opportunities to work with others to develop thinking on learning and teaching.**

From the discussions with middle leaders across 17 of the schools there emerged a number of dimensions to the role, which I've summarised under six headings below:

1. Delivering

- Own the department and take pride in its contribution
- Bring energy to what you do
- Manage the budget
- Plan short, medium and long term
- Be resolute when necessary.

2. Teaching

- Understand learning
- Identify components of both great learning and of great teaching
- Model high standards in your own teaching
- Know the students
- Observe others and give feedback on their teaching.

3. Buffering

- Soften the hierarchy
- Interpret and protect the school vision
- Be positive and have consistent values
- Establish and maintain orderly systems
- Communicate regularly and clearly.

4. Supporting

- Be on top of performance data
- Motivate yourself and others
- Involve others in decision making
- Develop yourself, others and the team
- Contribute to the life of the school.

5. Challenging

- Ask questions and encourage others to do so
- Direct and be directive when necessary
- Monitor performance
- Benchmark and model consistency and standards
- Challenge mediocrity.

6. Scanning

- Keep your specialist knowledge up to date
- Pioneer and set an example
- Be reflective
- Scan the horizon to understand what's possible
- Make informed and judicious decisions.

Recommendation for middle leaders: **look through the six dimensions of the role. Ask yourself to what extent are you pursuing each.**

14. Delivering: own what you do

We work together, we share things, we talk about the children, we're proud of what we do!

Middle Leader, Weydon School

Two years ago I was driving past the teachers' centre in Chorley, Lancashire late on a winter's afternoon. The centre was on my right and there were playing fields to the left. The playing fields swept up to a 1960s secondary school building. As I looked up, a giant sign stuck inside the windows of several adjoining classroom proclaimed, 'This is Geography'. I was impressed. It was the most visible landmark for miles around!

It's a given that middle leaders should take pride in their department, in what it offers and how it can enthuse young people about the learning which can take place there. At Haybridge School, where there is a very good maths department, reasons for studying maths are literally etched onto windows and built into the walls.

A really useful activity for you and your colleagues is to take time together to agree the benefits. What are the benefits to students of each subject? Take each subject in turn and agree three to five very specific benefits. Do this before buying in posters containing endorsements from the rich and famous, contacting alumni or sticking up success stories.

Once – as a staff – you are clear on the broad benefits, then agree how to sell the benefits to students. Try putting facts alongside faces: 'Last year's average starting salary for a graduate with a good degree in maths was £21,000'. This sort of 'fact' placed under a quality photograph of an ex-student helps sell the benefit. Lots of schools do this sort of thing but it's rarely personalised to this extent. The more the students can relate it to someone they know, a place they know or an event with which they are familiar, the more they can see the benefit. 'I met my girlfriend through an exchange visit to Germany. Thank goodness I learned the language, and we're getting married next year!'

Here are some general statistics used by St John the Baptist School:

- 93 per cent attendance and above will give you a 73 per cent chance of achieving 5A*–C in your GCSEs whatever your ability.

- Below 90 per cent will give you only a 27 per cent chance of achieving 5A*–C in your GCSEs whatever your ability.

- 90 per cent attendance sounds good but one day off in ten over five years is equal to 95 days, which is 19 weeks and equal to half a school year!!

- Average earnings of permanently excluded students are £9,000 against £32,000 of those who stay in school.

- If your attendance improves by 1 per cent, attainment improves by 5 to 6 per cent.

And here are some more shared by Professor Dylan Wiliam:

- Increased lifetime salary (13 per cent for a degree)

- Improved health (60 per cent reduction in ill health for a degree)

- Longer life (1.7 years of life per extra year of schooling).[27]

Once you have got the broader benefits of learning within that subject discipline – as opposed to doing the course or getting the qualification – it's then time to go through each topic you teach and do a similar exercise. What exactly are the benefits to the students of learning about this topic? How can you express those benefits in simple, easy-to share-language?

One suggestion is to use a piece of software called CrazyTalk. It can animate any picture of a face and it gives you the power to bring it to life with easy auto lip-sync. This means that on your whiteboard, screen or wall, Albert Einstein, Bill Gates or Charlie Chaplin can share the outcomes and sell the benefits at the start of your lesson.

Recommendation for middle leaders: **own the department and take pride in its contribution. Ensure your colleagues are clear on the wider benefits of the subjects taught and regularly share these with students as part of lessons.**

Middle leaders work in the engine room of the school. It's hard work. It's especially hard when you are pulled in two directions at once: serving the wider needs of the school; supporting the more immediate needs of staff in the department. To be at your best in helping the school and others, you need to be able to maintain balance in your life. People who feel good about who they are and what they do are better able to maintain balance. For most, this means being positive in how we think, positive in how we sustain relationships and positive about how we manage demands. Balance head, heart and health!

Assume the best in others. Frame the potentially irritating, everyday weaknesses of some of your colleagues by finding the positive intent behind them. If there's no positive intent then a harder conversation follows. Try hard to remain focused on solutions to avoid fixating on problems. Keep the relationships positive and professional. Follow the mantra we advocate for all teachers and 'separate the behaviour from the person'.

Prioritise what you do. Many managers use an A, B, C system where A is impactful and must be done, B may have impact and so should be done and C could be done. Often the As are the hardest so we spend time doing Cs. We feel good because we are busy but the C list never has the impact we need. Some middle leaders I know do this on a Sunday night. They look at the week ahead and prioritise what's coming up. With your priority list decide straight away how to deal with each item. It's a case of dump it, do it, delegate it or defer it.

At a personal level, build in reprieve for yourself: regular planned time away from stressful events. If it's not possible for this to be in a social context then it may be possible to have 20 minutes to yourself early each morning or in a slot when you take exercise alone. Sometimes building in a walk helps. As mentioned earlier, a number of schools have well-being targets as part of performance management. If it's not a direction your school wishes to take at a formal level it can still be done informally within your department.

Recommendation for middle leaders: bring energy to what you do. Keep yourself physically, intellectually, emotionally and spiritually attuned to the rigours of the role.

Responsibility over finance for middle leaders is as much about awareness of whole school costs and expenditures and how they and their colleagues can contribute to efficiencies as it is about managing their own, often small budgets.

Middle leaders manage their department or faculty budgets well, taking a responsible and realistic attitude to their own spending. The budgetary cycle should be predictable containing few if any surprises and this means that the scope for getting it wrong is limited. Nevertheless it is possible through maverick behaviour to commit to irregular purchases and so overspend. As a set of general rules:

- align with the school budgetary cycle
- share any information regarding expenditure or possible savings
- schedule in spending and track it throughout the year
- hit deadlines
- don't hold or hide pots of money and carry them over

- don't make commitments which cannot be met

- look for savings on such things as training fees and stay informed about exam entry costs for all your subjects

- look to gain revenue where you have facilities which can be hired out

- teachers in your team should either be teaching, on preparation, planning and assessment (PPA) time or on management time.

- accept that there are very high costs related to small teaching groups in the sixth form and so such costs have to be justified.

For those of you who wish to move to a school leadership post some understanding of whole school financial issues will become necessary. In truth, there is very little in most middle leader roles that prepares you for analysing a balance sheet and financial planning when the numbers have six figures. Some schools run sessions for heads of departments on understanding whole school finance. This is largely about raising awareness and securing providence but is also developmental.

Recommendation for middle leaders: **manage the budget. Take a responsible and realistic attitude to financial spending.**

Find the time or the means to step back so that you can detach yourself from the everyday preoccupations and get the bigger picture.

Try envisaging your perfect department. What would it be like? How would people feel? What would students be doing? What would be on offer? In solution-focused approaches an activity called Future Perfect involves envisioning an ideal state. By asking questions such as 'What will be different when the obstacle is overcome?' the obstacle is often pushed to the side and a different picture emerges. Add to this other questions such as 'What will be the first small signs that things are improving?' and before you know it the group is focusing on ways forward. Asking 'what else?' or 'anything else?' and repeating these questions helps focus in on the gist of the solution.

For some types of planning, space to think and address the wider issues is more important than an instant answer. For example, planning around the use of emerging technologies is never successful when it's ad hoc. A decision about the purchase of, for example, Flip Video cameras for the department needs to be preceded by a discussion as to how they will enhance the learning experience of the students. This requires the decision makers to have developed a shared appreciation of what comprises great learning experiences in their discipline. So to make a decision on hardware or software purchases or to decide on the use of an application needs a longer view. How would the resources acquired serve our wider needs and help us move towards Future Perfect?

It used to be that whoever did the timetable called the shots in a school; very soon it will be your technology, particularly the virtual learning environment, that shapes resource acquisition and deployment. We are moving away from outside providers coming in and 'doing' you a website. We are moving towards tools which allow your students and staff to go through your school-managed portal with a unique sign-in and access the free Web 2.0 products which are already out there in abundance. It will not be so cost prohibitive but it will be time consuming to make informed choices. Invest time wisely.

Recommendation for middle leaders: plan short, medium and long term. Effort put into preparation and planning yields considerable dividends downstream.

Giving advice to others is sometimes difficult for middle leaders in a context where it could be seen as undermining the status quo and collegiality of the department. The balance between directing, guiding, advising, even 'dropping careful hints' can be difficult to get right. Too much of one can shift the climate of the department. Sometimes how it's offered is not how it's received and many middle leaders default to informal collegiality rather than have an action imply a status difference or create a feeling of obligation.

In the more successful schools the middle leader load is eased to some degree where there are well-established management practices across the school. Where it's routine for others to come into classrooms and observe; where there's open exchange of ideas; where there's an expectation that we help each other improve, it's so much easier for a middle leader to give advice. In poorer schools the middle leader is too often positioned as the lead administrator for the subject, corralled into taking up defensive positions on behalf of colleagues. The monitoring dimension to the middle leader role is most difficult in such contexts.

In spring 2010 a friend and colleague took up a middle leader role in a large secondary school in Devon. He was advised by the senior deputy not to timetable Patsy (not her real name) – one of the older subject teachers in his new department – for last thing Tuesday or Thursday afternoons as that was when she liked to go out horse riding. Such situations ought to be rare but for many middle leaders their idealism will be tested as a consequence of walking into situations where others have failed to put proper expectations in place. It's then you have to be resolute.

Recommendation for middle leaders: be resolute when necessary. The role is demanding and at times requires considerable determination. Being resolute should not however be confused with being dogmatic or parochial.

15. Teaching: build from learning

Our students are change agents we have to understand how they learn and help each other be better teachers.

Middle Leader, Sandringham School

It takes about six or seven years for teachers to hone their classroom skills and be at their best. Research into the professional skills of clinical psychologists, surgeons, auditors and dentists suggests that after about six or seven years their technical abilities can peak and in some cases go into decline. After a while, experience gives you no significant advantage. Diminishing returns have set in. What appears to make the difference are top-ups of professional learning spaced over time. Understanding learning is at the core of our profession and so staying up to date and professionally informed about new approaches to, and understanding of, learning is key to keeping our skills honed. One of the great high wire performers, Phillipe Petit, is constantly reinventing himself as a performer.

> *I taught myself to do all the things you could do on a wire. I learned the backward somersault, the front somersault, the unicycle, the bicycle, the chair on the wire, jumping through hoops. But I thought, 'What is the big deal here? It looks almost ugly.' So I started to discard those tricks and to reinvent my art.[28]*

It's a privilege to be able to work closely with schools in helping them to develop their teachers. When I first started to do this 20 years ago some of the teachers had started their education before the Second World War, trained as teachers in the 1950s and started teaching in the early 1960s. These were the elders of the tribe and I frequently received a metaphorical beating from them. There was often resistance to training, even the idea of training, especially if it was led by an outsider. We would have behaviours ranging from sullen resentment to open hostility. It was hard work. Over the next 20 years the groups got younger and I got older. The hostility disappeared to be replaced by higher and higher expectations. Professionalism was lifting.

In the last five years or so schools have started to do more for themselves. Their understanding of learning has increased exponentially and so to has their understanding of how best to develop themselves. What I notice now is the youth of school staff — with many in promoted posts they would have had to wait years for in previous generations — and amongst the recently graduated teachers the impact of the national curriculum, testing, assessment changes and narrowed teacher training. The younger groups are equally enthusiastic, equally talented than previous generations, but less creative and more conformist. They are the first generation of teachers who were taught the national curriculum throughout their entire school years. Now they're teaching others. More and more know how to write schemes of work, assessment criteria and lesson plans but fewer and fewer seem to know how to respond if it goes wrong!

Some of what you will need to do as a middle leader is foster the creativity in your young staff. A starting point would be to know and understand the continuum of learning and teaching we discussed above.

Set up for yourselves the 'What is great learning?' activity. Try it at the 'universal' level first – ten signature characteristics that apply to great learning in any context. Then apply each characteristic to your own subject. Remember it's about learning not about passing exams. Try creating flip chart-size cartoons, one of great learners in your subject and another of poor learners in the subject. Frame them and stick them up in the corridor.

Learning is a permanent change in behaviour or thinking arising as a consequence of an experience or insight. Sometimes it comes from within and sometimes it has to come from outside. Have a departmental library of books about learning: this one you are reading could be the first! Some schools have a learning 'reading club' with excerpts from books or articles copied and shared between staff. Go to www.ted.com and download some of the great presentations you find there. They last only 20 minutes at most and include some of the world's great thinkers speaking about their discipline.

Recommendation for middle leaders: understand learning. Stay up to date and professionally informed about new approaches to and understanding of learning. Encourage colleagues to do the same.

At the start of the academic year agree with the department what constitutes an 'outstanding' lesson following the great learning discussions described above. Provide observable features of your own or use ours. Once an agreed approach to learning and teaching is established create a display that outlines these features and then have copies in every classroom to model practice and ensure that it is a constant reminder. Reinforce some of the more important elements by using the idea of student protocols for learning. We described some earlier above. Agree your own protocols if necessary, trial them across each of your classes and stick them up in your classrooms and post them onto the school website. Use students to voice the protocols as short videos. Put these on your intranet.

Ban activities that are about coercion and behaviour management before they are about learning. Replace them with more positive alternatives. Discuss and agree what they could be. Here's your starter ban list:

- Copying objectives as a starter activity
- Dictation either to transmit information or for its own sake
- Copying from any textbook
- Copying from the board
- Wordsearches
- Colouring in
- Illustrations as the learning product
- Posters
- Copying up a 'perfect' version
- Finishing off for homework
- Do 'ten more' for homework
- Worksheets that are photocopied pages from a textbook
- Study leave.

Have one-minute videos stored on the intranet as video openers for lessons to set the context of the topic and share best practice. Update these on a regular basis so that each member of staff has an opportunity to share an experience.

At the end of a development day or staff meeting spend the last two minutes getting everyone to write down how their lessons will improve as a result of the day or something they will try as a result of the meeting.

Divide the curriculum into chunks and assign each member of the department an area to reduce staff lesson planning. For example, one teacher prepares all lessons for Year 7 and shares them with the rest of the team. This means in principle a teacher plans fewer lessons and therefore produces higher quality resources. Ensure your most suitable teachers plan resources for the examined groups. This is the quality assurance as middle leader.

Finally ask, 'When we do things in the classroom how do they connect to our agreed learning principles? Can we track our principles into practice? Are we a learning department or a teaching department or are we both?'

Recommendation for middle leaders: identify components of both great learning and of great teaching. Ensure you and your colleagues understand that great teaching can only ever emerge from an understanding of learning.

> *You could not have a bigger contrast between this school and the last place. In my last school the head of department and the second took the top sets and left us to struggle. Here we work out what's best for the students.*
>
> Middle Leader, St John the Baptist School

Be strategic in how you deploy your staff. Break the following habits of mind regarding teacher deployment and option groups:

- all year groups are equally important so deserve equal access to the best teachers
- the key groups are the top sets
- the top sets must have the best teachers
- we must spread the 'bad ones' around to reduce their impact
- all sets should be equal in number
- C/D borderline has to be the priority
- we should all take turns
- Fred got a double first – he can only ever take the top sets
- we have to cover the entire syllabus in our teaching
- only the teacher should do the marking
- students should be the final arbiter of their own option choices
- A level teaching is more akin to university teaching than to GCSE
- Students grow up between leaving Year 11 and arriving at Year 12
- Liking the teacher is a legitimate reason for choosing a subject.

Dispensing with the old habits of mind allows fresh and innovative thinking so that students, not their teachers, get the best deal!

Put your best teachers with either the key classes or the most challenging. Decide strategically which are key: schools are judged on results so some of your discussion has to be about securing better passes for the largest number of children. As a middle leader teach the key groups yourself. Don't hog the best sets. Work with the person responsible for timetabling to ensure this is done before everything else. Focus on Year 11, Year 12 and Year 13. KS3 may be less crucial! If necessary, change the structure. Instead of sets 1, 2, 3, 4, 5 and 6 being taught simultaneously timetable 1, 2 and 3 in each half so the best teachers can teach two crucial groups.

Take the weakest or most difficult individuals out of classes and place them with the best or most appropriate teachers so that the majority will succeed. This will also ensure students are best placed and given every chance to perform to the best of their ability. Opt for larger numbers in the higher ability sets so that the teachers with more challenging classes have smaller numbers.

In one of our outlier schools they have a planned enrolment of 185 – which is seven form entry. Their set numbers in English from top down are 34, 34, 34, 28, 26, 19 and 10. Set six happens to be the key C/D borderline class. These have to be smaller so the teacher has the best chance of success! Try to find the money for smaller groups in English as 30 essays can take forever to mark and, even with good peer assessment, can be difficult to give good quality feedback on.

Schools are measured by results. In turn, departments are measured in a similar way by the school. Consequently, with exam groups there is a need to train students to pass the exam, not necessarily to cover the entire syllabus. Peer marking of examination questions, peer feedback, paired discussions of model answers, exemplar materials and students talking to each other about success strategies all ensure students know the standards they are aspiring to. Make this part of everyday *exam group* teaching.

Recommendation for middle leaders: **model high standards in your own teaching. Be strategic in how you deploy the talent in your department.**

At Walthamstow School some of the staff meetings are preceded by a scrolling PowerPoint slide showing pictures of students who fall into the category for discussion. It may be that these are girls who are on free school meals or who are bringing behavioural challenges or who have English as an additional language. On other occasions photographs are circulated to stimulate informal conversations and to ensure no girl is overlooked.

For each subject group provide their teacher with a set of laminated A6 cards each of which has a photograph of the student alongside their name. These cards can be used for a number of purposes and are a great asset. Teachers love them for their simplicity. They can be used for learning names, creating seating plans, ensuring that rewards are balanced and appropriate, personalising provision, distributing classroom roles or tasks fairly and randomising questions.

Electronic random name generators are also useful for ensuring that attention is distributed equitably amongst each class. They can be downloaded easily. Make sure all the names are included.

Depending on which of the above you prefer, more data – perhaps related to past performance and future potential – can be added to each card. Have a duplicate set of each and have these on permanent display in your office space and on your intranet. The cards can be used in review meetings so that you discuss individuals and not groups or categories within groups. Where there are significant health issues or safeguarding issues the information can be coded and added to the cards.

As an alternative, remove or limit performance and future potential data from the cards and replace it with unique qualities information: likes, dislikes, interests and aspirations of the student. Now you can have informed conversations, personalise the learning, move groups around and arrange seating plans on a different basis.

Be very clear with colleagues on what information about students is a must-have and what must be known about each indvidual.

When discussing students, focus on what's best for the student. For example, be really careful with Year 10 and Year 12 options that you aren't setting up a weak child to fail. Who is in charge of making sure this doesn't happen in your school? A boy with low levels of concentration choosing French because he liked the teacher in Year 9 can disrupt the entire group in Year 11.

If you have a small enough number put the most difficult students all in one group and ensure they have outstanding teachers every lesson. It saves hundreds of hours of leadership and pastoral time spent mopping up after a weak teacher.

Have a 'cockerel club'. Any children late to school on any day are phoned at home between 7 a.m. and 8 a.m. the following day to make sure they are up and ready for school.

Personalise correspondence home. Check to the last detail essential things such as the correct and full spelling of names. Send as many praise letters as you send concern letters! When you send a concern letter attach some support strategies for the parents that have been agreed by the subject team and accessed via the intranet. Far better to take time out as a team to identify the most common issues shared in letters of concern to parents than to reinvent a letter each time or, worse, send home a standard letter which will be badly received. Agree some simple, positive and practical guidance that benefits all parties and can go home and fit to the student. You could do the same with praise letters, for example: 'Alistair is doing really well but to support and ensure he's even more successful you may want to ...'

Recommendation for middle leaders: know the students. Make it a professional obligation to know who they are. As students move into exam groups ensure that you and your colleagues have detailed profiles of past performance, future potential and unique qualities.

Middle leaders tend to show great resistance to the idea of monitoring the quality of their colleagues' work, especially by observing them in the classroom. Observation is seen as a challenge to professional norms of equality and privacy, and sometimes as an abrogation of trust. Subject leaders who managed to introduce some sort of classroom observation procedure did so as a collaborative learning activity for the entire department rather than as a management activity for the subject leader.

To get better outcomes from observations start by using the ten fundamentals of great learning ideas described earlier. Once you have your own fundamentals agreed and itemised coherence of approach can quickly follow. Here are some more suggested uses to follow on from those listed earlier:

- Website summary. Place your list prominently on your school website so that staff, students and most importantly parents can see it. Very few schools share anything to do with learning with parents. It's a classic error: how can they help their child if they have no more than a basic understanding of what it means to learn well? Also make sure that if you have plasma television screens networked together around the school that the list appears on those too.

- Staff planner. Use the staff planner to annotate a copy of the classroom prompt poster explaining the thinking behind each feature and a little about how to use it as a classroom teaching resource.

- Learning review observation checklist. This is where your school can align with inspection criteria. For each of your features define what satisfactory, good, outstanding and beyond outstanding looks like. Write the features in easy-to-follow descriptors noting the changes between each category. I've included an example of one we use in the appendices.

- Observation sheet. We use an electronic version called L2 Observe. It cuts down on the hundreds of pieces of paper which float around after observations and which can be impenetrable. It also allows for instant analysis of data. For those who prefer the paper keep it as simple and end user-friendly as possible.

- Learning review staff questionnaire. For each feature provide a question with either an open ended response or a yes and no response. I've attached an example of one we use in the appendices.

- Learning review student questionnaire. Again, provide a question with either an open-ended response or a yes and no response. This lends itself to an online version such as those possible using SurveyMonkey. I've included an example of the paper version we use in the appendices.

- Learning review peer observation prompt. Take each feature and in consultation with your colleague decide which will be the focus of your observation. The feedback is not about overall inspection grades but is to do with the specific area of focus.

- Learning walk prompt. Take each feature and alongside add either a simple yes or no or contrasting adjectives such as active/passive. For each it can be a simple tick or use of a highlighter to indicate the impression given. Too many schools dismiss this opportunity. Chafford uses a marking system and claims a really tight correlation between the 1s and 2s recorded on the learning walks and the outcomes in that subject. The best teachers and best departments consistently score higher.

Take time with colleagues to design simple observation and review systems that will support you. Focus on professional development, not on grading.

Recommendation for middle leaders: observe others and give feedback on their teaching. Shift the culture. Go beyond performance management to create shared opportunities to plan, teach, observe each other and review for improvement.

Some schools are working on applications (or apps) for some of the above processes. The day can't come quickly enough! The amount of paper consumed by schools is phenomenal! Typically a large secondary school uses a pallet of paper a week. Many lesson observation sheets suffer from poor design requiring a great deal of concentration and effort on the part of the observer and even more by anyone who then has to interpret and collate the outcomes.

A typical example of an observation sheet is a side or two of A4, either portrait or landscape, usually with summary details of the lesson observed at the top, a small box for a grade O/G/S/N then boxes for written observations around the strengths of the lesson, what went well, what was the evidence of progress with the key factors influencing this progress and a small box at the bottom entitled 'areas for development'. There are tiny spaces in which to write and consequently lots of scope for oversight, omissions and value judgements with high levels of partiality.

Underneath or alongside this there is often some sort of criteria. In the two examples of observation schedules I have in front of me now there are separate checklists, one for learning and one for teaching, with anything between 9 and 13 items in each.

By separating learning and teaching within observations we create a dislocation. There are a number of issues around the design of observation systems that are worth all schools looking at in some detail.

Firstly, be clear on the *purpose*. Who and what is it for? If it's for accountability, an evidence base for external inspection and to benchmark grades then it is designed and used differently than one for development, sharing of good practice and to plan for improvements. There ought to be no checklists that are only ever seen or referred to on observation sheets! So if those 9 and 13 bullet points only ever appear in that precise format on an observation sheet it begs the question about the value of each list. Ensure that what you observe against has emerged from an agreed whole school view on what constitutes great learning otherwise it's box ticking for inspectors!

Secondly, ask hard questions about the *practicality* of the exercise. If you have 100 members of staff each observed once annually for let's say 45 minutes with a 15-minute debriefing, that's 100 hours before any sort of analysis has yet taken place. Add in six minutes of analysis each – as much as you typically get at the doctors – and that's 110 hours. Over three years, that's a minimum of 55 working days committed to a paper-based accountability exercise! Better make sure it helps!

Finally ensure the *product* for end users is worthwhile. Observations that are based on a common understanding of what is being observed, how the observations are identified, collated and then used, plus an opportunity to use the feedback to inform future behaviour is the very minimum one would expect.

It really is worth looking at simplifying the observation system so that outcomes can be collated easily, added to a numeric database and summarised at the touch of a button. The fewer hands it goes through the better! I've yet to see a school that is using a really simple, hands-on electronic observation and review system. I guess that's why we developed our own!

With only 50 staff, the lesson observation target for the year at Chafford is 300 peer-led reviews.

Recommendation for middle leaders: **design or obtain a customisable electronic observation system to avoid storing and transferring information from hundreds of sheets of paper.**

16. Buffering: soften the hierarchy

Part of what we do is interpret and protect the school vision, what it is we stand for.

Middle Leader, Haybridge School

The middle leader acts as a buffer between subject-specialist colleagues and the school leadership. It's not unlike being the interpreter and the diplomat rolled into one. In a complex and ongoing international negotiation you must be trilingual – be fluent in each of management, department and subject. Part of your job is to make it easier for others to do their job.

Softening the hierarchy also means you helping out. Across the schools there were many examples of middle leaders who took time to relieve staff during their free periods if they were having a particularly stressful time. Quietly and progressively removing jobs from staff under pressure without them noticing was another means of spreading the load.

There are many schools that recognise they play a role in helping staff stay at their best. For some middle leaders this may mean intervening when junior and less experienced teachers are getting things out of balance. In one of our outlier schools a young teacher was very distressed about workload and from time to time would stay up all night marking books and preparing lessons. This led inevitably to exhaustion and stress. Before it could get worse the department head physically removed all exercise books and the school laptop from the teacher's bag then sent him home for the weekend on Friday at 5 p.m. Just after 6 p.m. that same evening the young teacher was caught sneaking back into school and was marched off the premises before he could get to his marking! Absence through stress benefits no one.

Recommendation for middle leaders: soften the hierarchy. Part of your job is to make it easier for others to do their job. Monitor and help manage the workload of your colleagues, especially those who are less experienced.

What is the school vision and how does it apply to your school? At Weydon School the core purpose of 'Inspiring Minds' is used as a theme for assemblies across the school, it's discussed at meetings and prompted through staff briefings.

If you are a head teacher every nuance of what is said – either in public or in conversation – gets picked over and interpreted. This is especially so in challenging times. As a middle leader it is very easy to get sucked into talking about personalities, speculation and hearsay. Try to avoid putting decisions you find hard to communicate into the mouths of others! Avoid displacing responsibility or using the killer phrases! Here are some I've encountered over the years. How would you expect others to respond?

- 'Management – in their wisdom – have decided …'
- 'They have told me to tell you …'
- 'This has just been given to me …'
- 'I'm no wiser than you are on this one …'
- 'Same old story …'
- 'You'll never believe this but …'
- 'I don't like having to do this …'
- 'It wouldn't have been my choice …'
- 'I don't know all the facts but in my view …'
- 'In my last school …'
- 'Don't shoot the messenger …'

The fish rots from the head. The concept of shared responsibility becomes difficult when schools are in challenging circumstances, have weak or no leadership or suffer high levels of turbulence. For a middle leader this is hard because you have conflicts of loyalty. In some contexts colleagues know this and some exploit it. A young and relatively inexperienced middle leader may have all the status but none of the power. The role can be undermined by colleagues operating in cliques, emphasising their experience at the expense of yours or questioning your loyalties. Never go into a bear pit without a plan and without a few trusted friends! Before all your meetings, decide what is the best outcome for students, how any suggested changes can best impact on students and how colleagues can best pull together to secure what's needed.

Recommendation for middle leaders: interpret and protect the school vision. Be supportive of the school leadership team as far as is possible. Stay appraised of the facts, don't speculate about intentions or encourage others to do so.

As a middle leader you will spend a lot of time in meetings. It's easy to be cynical about meetings but there are behaviours that will undermine any meeting and behaviours that lead to success. Treat meetings as staff development opportunities where you and colleagues can practise the skills we ask of students. We ask students to collaborate, focus on task, complete the task and do so in a positive supportive atmosphere. Why not ask the same of each other in meetings? Try developing these behaviours:

- Clear outcomes. Write them up so everyone can see them. Put a time frame on them. 'If we are successful by 5.30 p.m. we will have ...'

- Prioritise items based on agreed criteria. Allocate more time to key items and discuss them early. If necessary go through the agenda at the beginning and prioritise it against A, B, C.

- Record actions. Use a flip chart to record actions and put a name to each: 'Alistair will bring the document to the next meeting and circulate it two days beforehand ...'

- Communicate well. Ask great questions, clarify, build on the ideas of others, summarise, paraphrase and invite views.

- Conclude feeling good! Sort out disagreements there and then. Secure the outcomes you wrote up earlier. Agree actions and leave with a feeling of having done something worthwhile.

In October 2010 I facilitated the World Cup review on behalf of the Football Association. This was a two-day residential involving representatives from the professional game. There were 85 individuals – all of whom had something to say and many of whom were understandably disappointed at the national team's performance in the 2010 World Cup in South Africa and agitated as a consequence. To have one large meeting was to court disaster. We opted for small groups following specialised interests, which then fed into the main theme and a larger meeting. To keep things on track we used yellow cards for offences such as talking over someone, straying off the point, waffling, answering a question with an answer to a different question and wandering aimlessly down memory lane. Red cards were used on repeat offenders! Keep your meetings focused and if possible do so with a light touch!

Recommendation for middle leaders: **be positive and have consistent values. Focus on solutions, encourage others to do the same.**

The sorts of interventions, structures and systems used by every department and headed up by middle leaders include:

- Effective meetings. Make sure you limit their number and frequency. Focus on student outcomes and learning in each and prioritise items. Consider making all your scheduled meetings development meetings and do the administrative tasks informally.

- Schemes of work. Cited in every school as making a difference when they were thought through carefully, accessible and in place.

- Lesson plans. Based on a model of learning.

- Observation schedules. Both performance and development observations.

- Marking policies. Light-touch marking and marking that involves students pairs of students and groups of students in addition to the teacher. Pursue a balance of electronic and paper-based feedback.

- Book scrutiny. Have a guaranteed turnaround on marking of two weeks. Check this is happening. It's the tail that wags the monitoring dog!

- Handbooks. A big one for policies and procedures, contractual and legal stuff. A teacher friendly smaller planner with key dates, deadlines, data and learning stuff!

- Seating plans. Agreed approaches to room layout for learning. At St John the Baptist School they use seating plans with the target grade written on them saying it really helps differentiation.

- Student targets. Everyone clear about individual student targets including above, at and below.

- Student data. Not only are staff in possession of the data, they know its significance, where it comes from and how it stands up in comparison to others.

- Communication strategies. Minimise the amount of paper and emails sent around the system. For example, introduce systems that filter out staff using the subject box: DELETE IF YOU DO NOT TEACH Y7.

- Behaviour policies. Best written as bullet point summaries with versions for students, staff, administrative staff and parents.

- Rewards and praise systems. Simple, easy to administer and balanced. Don't overwork these systems. Their value is overestimated. The best rewards are the accolades of your peers and the ongoing interest of your teachers.

- Quality assuring reports and correspondence. Anything that goes home has to be spot on. Any point at which the school, its students or staff interface with the public has to be spot on.

Recommendation for middle leaders: **establish and maintain orderly systems. Ensure that everyone is well informed about and understands the agreed working practices.**

Be visible to all. Make sure you get to lessons to find out what is going on. This is your quality assurance and your communication strategy. A scheme of work is neither a guarantee of any sort of teacher quality nor is it a quality assurance tool. If you see something outstanding in someone's lesson follow up by sending an email, a note or try to have a quick conversation. Personal 'thank yous' are very powerful for building relationships.

Middle leaders in the more successful schools kept communication as simple as possible. Some provided a one-side daily briefing sheet though a weekly equivalent was more common. A flip-chart summary of things to be done or remembered which is positioned in your departmental office for all to see is often better than lots of separate memos. Limit the paper used.

Include your learning support assistants and others attached to your department – such as trainee teachers – in all communications. Provide a departmental calendar for the key moments in the year, particularly those impacting on exam groups.

Use your departmental mini-handbook as a means of putting the everyday practical information in front of the team, sharing systems and procedures. Keep it simple and useful. It's a great way of maintaining consistency.

Recommendation for middle leaders: **communicate regularly and clearly. Publish the yearly cycle. Run all meetings with clear outcomes and action points. Use a departmental handbook as a reference and resource. Maintain it as a working document.**

17. Supporting: track performance

Staff, the girls, the parents, we all know baseline, working at and target levels or grade – when the data is good there's no arguments.

Middle Leader, St Angela's School

Whilst the school needs to be on top of all student performance data and middle leaders on top of the department data, the subject teachers need to have some of it filtered out. Provide access in two categories: *must have* and *must know*. Must have needs to be at the teacher's fingertips constantly. Must know needs to be easily accessible should the teacher need it. Collating the data is a key role so as middle leader you either do this or liaise with your school data geek so that you have what you need.

Don't give teachers a raft of information about students – just the targets they need to deliver on – then make sure they know and use them. Ensure that the grade you set will deliver positive contextual value added (CVA), and more recently Ofsted are keen on the percentage of students who make three levels of progress so take this into account. Work out where the department is gaining or losing value added – which classes, which teachers and students. Share the results. Poor performance in one class will drag the whole department's results down. Link the data to a set of stepped interventions, so that all staff know what has triggered a particular strategy.

Most schools will have must have data showing above, below or on target for each student. At St Angela's they can very quickly provide must know data including what they call stickmen performance graphs of each student and whether they have regressed or are stuck, slow moving or fast moving. The must know data includes SAT, CAT, Fischer Family Trust, RAISEonline and CVA. Performance can be monitored against prior attainment and against attainment of previous groups. The school provides staff with 'frequent snapshots' in an attempt to inform the connection of staff, students and parents.

Students at St Angela's also access some of their own must have data through 'the level-headed campaign', which displays sub-levels in each subject and is displayed in classrooms.

In two schools in the project there was the equivalent of a 'war room' with a large Venn diagram with photos of children who need additional support on it. Some schools get the heads of maths and English to share an office so they know and discuss the targeted students.

If a teacher in your department doesn't deliver on results do you look them in the eye and tell them it's not good enough? You would be surprised how common it is to avoid doing this, passing the responsibility upwards or deferring the moment. Sometimes middle leaders will write a report excusing poor results in the hope that the report will be the end of the issue rather than the beginning of the discussion. Put the students first. If it's happening now it's highly likely that if nothing changes, it will happen again in the future.

Finally, in one of our schools the head teacher suggested adding ten points to every student's CAT score before they joined the school and not telling anyone!

Recommendation for middle leaders: be on top of performance data. Use data to drive department thinking about pupil performance and interventions. Ensure everyone understands the significance of data and can explain its relevance in simple terms to parents and pupils.

> *Every assessment is recorded in science, every module, every test – it's all data tracked. The nature of so many GCSEs means that thousands of bits of data are flying around. You could lose 10 per cent and it would be a disaster – data management is a large part of my job.*

> Middle Leader, Tudor Grange

You cannot afford to compromise on standards. It's easier to stay motivated when there is strong buy-in from all the team to core purpose, when your systems and structures are simple and helpful, when there is a team ethos and a sense of collective improvement. One analysis of effective middle-leader behaviours described a department that was asked about its excellent results. The comment reiterated in the technology team meeting and in individual interviews was: 'We plod, but it is consistent plod.'

My working definition of motivation is: 'Motivation equals opportunity plus expectation times value'. If you share this with colleagues you can try applying it to each of your subject disciplines and to your students. What do we do to motivate each other? What can we do better or differently to motivate our students?

Recommendation for middle leaders: motivate yourself and others. It's easier to stay motivated when there is strong buy-in to core purpose, when systems and structures are simple and helpful, when there is a team ethos and a sense of collective improvement. Motivation isn't about one-off speeches!

It's not always possible to reach shared agreement, but it's always desirable to use a shared process. Involve others in decision making wherever possible. It can be used as a mechanism for dealing with issues and building morale.

Try using an impact versus do-ability graph. Have your team take a challenge they face. Write out the challenge so all can see it. Then get individuals to generate as many alternative solutions on Post-it notes as they can in five minutes. As the solutions are written up, stick each note on to a flip chart. Keep writing and generating solutions. When this phase is complete rank each solution from one to four for impact and for do-ability. Five is highly impactful and also very easy to implement. Score the items and lay them out in a table. Transfer the items onto a graph with do-ability on the Y axis and impact on the X axis. Focus only on those solutions towards the top right-hand corner that have high impact and are easy to do.

Another approach involves sitting the person who owns the challenge in a chair and others face the chair and can only ask questions! No advice, no comparisons, no comments – only questions. The assumption being that the person will eventually reach his or her own conclusions.

Team problem solving takes place when we all focus on one problem and follow a shared method of problem solving. It is really powerful when middle leaders can use the same method as their students to address school- or department-wide issues. Use techniques such as the TASC Wheel, the Thinking Hats or the Kipling Questions.[29]

Involve students in shadowing your department. In some schools students are attached to departments and act as subject envoys – attending meetings, helping design lessons, writing up subjects blogs, maintaining parts of the website and being available to talk to parents and other students on options evenings.

Recommendation for middle leaders: involve others in decision making. It's not always possible to reach shared agreement, but it's always desirable to use a shared process.

Get away from thinking about continuous professional development being about finding and going on a suitable course. Seek a balance of professional learning and development models to avoid over-reliance on one type of provision. As a middle leader you must share responsibility for developing the all-round abilities and knowledge base of your team. You cannot do this just by going on courses or waiting for a good inset day.

In each of the project schools I asked the following questions about CPD: 'What is the school approach to professional development? How do you address any unevenness in the professional abilities and motivation of staff?'

There was considerable variety in the ambition, quality and scope of continuous professional development across the schools. It was another signifier of difference in the participants' school cultures. In some of the schools it was ad hoc, short term, pragmatic, course based, 'expert' led and co-ordinator initiated. For example, in response to the questions above, one school middle leader talked, with a degree of uncertainty, about which 'courses were available'.

In others there was a long-term approach, based on a coaching or peer development culture and closely linked to school development planning. In these schools it was carefully planned, costed, personalised and accredited, with a balance of tacit and formal inputs. In between these two extremes were a number of different approaches, which could be characterised as 'a bit of a mixed bag'.

At St Richard's what they call the personal and professional development programme is generated from an evaluation audit that takes place in July of each year, their college development plan requirements and feedback from the performance management cycle. There are three types of professional provision:

- Training – including courses and specific activities

- Support – includes coaching, mentoring and in-role support

- Education – includes research and higher qualifications.

In addition, the college encourages staff to try something new in a programme they call personal learning.

For your departmental CPD make sure you have the following principles in place:

- CPD is valued

- CPD is about both skills and knowledge

- Our return on the investment should be improved experiences for students

- Nothing goes out that doesn't come back and can be used by our community

- CPD is ongoing and not a one-off

- There is a long-term vision behind CPD which is linked to our school and departmental planning

- CPD goes beyond the expedient and need to know

- CPD is recognised either through accreditation or validation by school

- We review and evaluate CPD as a matter of course.

At the JFS School there is an enrichment programme with several tracks, including one for more experienced teachers who may enjoy and benefit from a 'sort of refresher programme', which focuses on innovative approaches to learning and assessment.

At Chafford Hundred Campus 90 per cent of all staff are on some sort of accredited training programme. For example, classroom assistants are all level two counsellor trained and 40 staff have been on international placements. The continuous professional development budget was one of only three that went up in real terms in the last year and it has more than doubled in the last five years. At the school, staff get all their gain time, there is no cover.

At Sandringham one inset day has been disaggregated into six hours to be run as twilight sessions throughout the year. Each member of staff has to choose six one-hour sessions to attend, some of which are mandatory and some of which are optional. These are run in-house to fit around both the school learning and teaching focus as well as staffing needs. They are called 'Teaching Toolkit' sessions and the school leadership team, advanced skills teachers and staff on upper pay spine three run the sessions. The school also pays staff from other schools to run sessions where it represents value for the investment.

Haybridge School has a very structured and thought-through approach to continuous professional development. Some of the features include:

- Integration with the school development plan priorities in a two-way relationship. The 'big ideas' which emerge from the SDP are interpreted by departments and the departments in turn 'feed up' their own suggested priorities

- Utilising the 360-degree feedback provided by staff

- Each year there will be a whole school 'push' on an agreed issue – most recently it has been passivity in sixth-form lessons

- Training days are very structured

- Linked into training with the Wyre Forest consortium of seven schools

- Staff meetings are developmental, there are none which are information driven. All start with teaching 'butterflies' – small things which have a big impact

- Departments conduct their own observations

- Lots of support and development for support staff

- Junior teachers have a weekly meeting with their subject mentor

- NQTs have monthly meetings with others in the consortium schools

- Visit programme to other specialist schools to look at ideas such as co-operative learning or using the staffroom as a learning centre

- Some set courses are in place in the school and as part of the consortium including Emergent Leaders and Leading from the Middle. All staff do the Emergent Leaders course

- For agreed external courses, which tend to be subject based, the school funds 50 per cent of the cost or provides a contribution of up to £500

- There is a staff reading board which provides material to do with issues around learning and teaching

- Monday school leadership team meetings start with shared reading and the breakfast meeting on Friday is business.

At Seven Kings there are 42 qualified coaches who have all been trained by the advanced skills teachers. Their recently qualified teacher programme starts with the skills of coaching so when they subsequently do training in classroom methods such as higher order thinking or assessment for learning they can coach each other.

Introduce a coaching approach within your department or, if a full-scale approach is not practical, use your department meetings to practise the techniques.

Recommendation for middle leaders: seek a balance of professional learning and development models to avoid over-reliance on one type of provision. Introduce a coaching approach.

At St Paul's School in Haywards Heath the team of eight 'lead learners' set out to improve the levels of student engagement in lessons across the school. Part of the strategy was to encourage colleagues to adopt a learning cycle – connect/outcomes/activate/demonstrate/consolidate – to help plan lessons. It was also to encourage them to take more risks with their teaching. The lead learners were keen to bolster up peer observation and support.

They decided to share the planning of lessons in 'unlikely' pairs. For example, the lead learner who was a maths teacher would lead the planning on a music lesson and the lead learner who was a music teacher on a maths lesson. They would then deliver the lesson and so model the process. The thinking here was to encourage the view that designing engaging learning experiences was firstly dependent on understanding the fundamentals of learning, then it was about being clear on the outcomes and then finally about structuring experiences into a lesson plan based on the learning cycle. Detailed subject knowledge, whilst important, was not necessarily the whole story with regard to effective classroom practice.

Create a directory of all the talents to inform peer observations. Walthamstow School for Girls combines a directory of good practice with staff names and their specialism with a peer observation voucher system. The voucher goes to each member of staff who can then choose who to observe. The voucher is then attached to the cover request slip.

At Thornden the school has a learning and teaching observation cycle with four types of observation:

1. Lesson observations conducted by line managers

2. Peer observations involving all teaching staff

3. Learning walks involving all teaching staff

4. Senoir management team observations.

All Thornden staff do peer observations and/or learning walks to look at and highlight good practice, share good practice, encourage reflection and contribute to whole school CPD. Recently, when the school was closely linked with a partner school, the entire school staff were shadowed by staff from another school who looked at either a topic within a subject, a departmental activity or had an opportunity to track a year group.

Being part of a project that funded links with other schools had helped smooth out any unevenness in the quality of teaching. Encourage colleagues to get into each other's lessons more. If there are no school improvement groups then create your own department improvement groups.

Recommendation for middle leaders: **develop yourself, others and the team. Actively seek formal and informal opportunities inside and outside of school to enhance the professional capabilities of your staff. Where possible give responsibility as part of development.**

For a lot of staff here, their life is the school – you have to have a life beyond the school so the students can see that you're human!

Teacher, Tudor Grange School

People who feel good about who they are and what they do, contribute more. According to Barbara Frederickson productivity in work environments is linked to mood.[30] People who are in positive moods generate more ideas, think strategically and see the bigger picture.

One of the project questions asked of every school was about the school as a community. 'What does the school celebrate with most enthusiasm? Who gets involved? What are the key points in the school year? What brings people together?' This was in an attempt to further gauge the 'cohesiveness' of the school. I was intrigued by the possibility of a school staff buying in heavily to the core purpose of the school leading to significant cohesion and therefore much more success. Some of the research on positive psychology helps us understand the worth of positive environments:

- Negative emotions facilitate highly focused, defensive critical thinking and decision making whereas positive emotions facilitate creative tolerant thinking and productivity

- Positive environments lead to improved problem solving. Frederickson and Branigan[31] found that a neutral mood state would typically generate 12 new ideas, a joyous state 14 and an angry state 7

- Happier people are more productive. In a study of over 200 workers over an 18-month period happier people obtained better evaluations and more pay awards than their unhappier counterparts

- A positive outlook is good for one's health and leads to reduced absenteeism. In a study of several hundred healthy volunteers who were administered nasal drops containing a common cold virus, the more positive the emotional style of the volunteers, the lower the risk of developing a cold

- Children with positive mood states learn faster.

In project schools debate and discussion around core purpose seemed to offer a route to social and professional cohesiveness. In each of the project schools I had fully anticipated encountering staff who knew each other well, who were comfortable in each other's company, who enjoyed the energy of the group and who would rely on the group in adverse times. I had also conjectured beforehand that tight cohesion would make whole school approaches to change easier to implement and make coping with crisis easier. I was therefore surprised at the very mixed picture with regard to the social cohesiveness of each school.

Where schools were vertical in organisation with 'strong semi-autonomous' departments, whole school developments were less evident. In these, relationships were more businesslike, with planned and formal social interactions. In other schools social interaction was more ad hoc, more vibrant and inclusive. Leadership style, school structure, travel time to work and the geography of the site played a significant part in shaping cohesiveness.

Ensure that your celebratory activities, social events and informal get-togethers are inclusive.

Recommendation for middle leaders: contribute to the life of the school. Departments can become isolated especially in larger schools. Encourage colleagues to take on whole school initiatives and opportunities.

18. Challenging: ask the right questions

We're constantly challenging ourselves to get better. You would not survive five minutes in this school if you weren't on it night and day!

Middle Leader, Chafford Hundred Campus

Some departments, like some schools, never reflect. They go on and on and on – and do so by staying well within their comfort zone. In these circumstances nothing will ever change.

In order to get better you must be prepared to ask the hard questions. Hard questions usually upset the equilibrium. This can be useful in instances when a school or department is coasting. However a 'coasting' situation may have arisen because it has not been within the culture to ask questions of what's already in place and seemingly successful. If as a middle leader you recognise the need to challenge complacency don't wade in without creating the right 'micro-climate' first. The right micro-climate is one where colleagues feel a sense of worth, see themselves as making a positive contribution and are positioned now to look at what might make *us* even better.

To get to this position may require the support of the school leadership team perhaps through an endorsement of a rolling programme of departmental reviews or the creation of a 'blue sky thinking' day. Some schools accelerate the process by having a 'if we were to start from scratch what would it look like?' event. For many schools the Building Schools for the Future programme precipitated a headlong rush into this sort of thinking. Whatever it takes, get your colleagues feeling they own the activity before asking any hard questions! When you do ask the hard questions they may look like these:

- Are our lessons actually worth behaving for?

- Why does our timetable never change? How many different timetables are worth considering in any academic year?

- Why does school start at the same time for everyone?

- Should specialists take all the exam groups?

- Would gap year students be a better option than teachers to help with A level support?

- Can we create supergroups by combining sets and giving them high quality lectures with follow up support?

- What do we do on a regular basis that does not contribute to improving learning? How soon will we abandon such practices?

- What's wrong with mobiles in lessons? Why not introduce them in Year 10?

- Should the department have a Facebook account?

- Should we all be on Twitter?

- Can we put revision tips on YouTube? What about lesson starters?

- Do we allow coursework to be submitted that is less than the target grade?

- What proportion of PE lessons need a gym? What proportion of science lessons need a lab?

- Have we provided parents with a booklet of work for each subject for when their child says there is no homework?

- How useful to a parent is a raw grade or score for effort?

- In what ways does a grade for behaviour reflect the student's capacity and willingness to learn?

- Many schools spend 100 hours per year on registration. How do we use it?

- Why do we do so few lesson observations? Ten observations a year is still only 1 per cent of anyone's teaching. Most people can turn it on for an observation but it's what happens day in day out that counts.

- How productive are our assemblies? Why not have learning assemblies or motivational assemblies for different groups in Years 10 and 11?

As a matter of course we should be reflecting on our professional practice. The opportunity to question some of our more cherished practices needs to be positioned as a positive collegiate activity otherwise it becomes sniper training for cynics.

Recommendation for middle leaders: ask questions and encourage others to do so. Use departmental meetings and discussions as an opportunity to use some of the questioning and thinking techniques you would use in lessons.

If you are going on an abseiling course that culminates in running down the side of a 200 foot cliff, you want to be told what to do. If the instructor puts you into small groups to socially construct a solution, wait for your opportunity and run for it! There are some situations where you just have to be told!

Most teachers come into the profession filled with good intent. For a tiny handful that good intent gets lost along the way. They are no longer the idealists they once were. Teaching is difficult in this situation. When it's only a job, that drive in the morning becomes harder. Energy seeps away at the margins. This does not make the person bad; it may have left them cynical, difficult and disruptive. But deep down there is still a desire to do what's right. In such circumstances most people want, and are liberated by, the truth. Susan Scott, in her book *Fierce Conversations*, quotes the statement, 'The person who can most accurately describe reality without assigning blame will emerge the leader.' [32] There's your challenge!

Here's some guidance on how you might survive a fierce conversation:

- Prepare by thinking through how you will calmly pursue your outcome

- Choose the right time and place; clear the decks

- Maintain the dignity of each of you throughout

- Agree what you want in very broad terms – 'it would be good to get a way forward on this ...' it's best to frame an outcome in terms of benefits to students

- Tackle the biggest challenges first

- Deal with the reality but describe the reality in facts not opinions

- Slow things down

- Ask questions and listen

- Tell it like it is, don't hide behind euphemisms

- Stay fully engaged with the current conversation

- Keep the focus on outcomes and not on personalities

- Clarify and summarise as you go

- Agree an action or set of actions to take the situation forward

- End on a positive – affirm what's been agreed.

If you're the head of department there are no trivial comments; own your emotional trail. Think of how the head teacher's words are interpreted by staff after each briefing. There's no value in loose talk.

Walthamstow School for Girls train middle leaders in having difficult conversations, reminding them of the mafia code that 'it's business and not personal'. The leadership style is deliberately collegiate, staff get involved in agreeing all the main policies, but there is also a willingness to confront the brutal facts. Leaders in the school help this process by acknowledging the difficulties in confronting under-performance and by openly admitting their own vulnerabilities.

Recommendation for middle leaders: be direct if necessary. Sometimes there are occasions that require a fierce conversation.

You get a pat on the back for five minutes and then it's 'now let's move on'.

Middle Leader, Haybridge

If, as a middle leader, you find yourself in a review meeting with school leadership in September trying to justify a set of results that caught you by surprise, you are not doing your job! We're not talking about individual marking anomalies. If you have class sets which have gone untracked, had no intervention, arrived unprepared and failed at the exam hurdle, you are at fault.

The progress and results of any colleague or any student in your department should never be a surprise. With proper data, close controls, regular reviews and a climate of openness, there should never be sleepless nights in September. Write it up large in your office! Give yourself a chance to intervene early, move staff around, change the configuration of groups, add booster and catch-up classes or Saturday clubs, assign mentors or beef up classroom teaching. Remember – no surprises!

The quality of what your teachers do matters to a degree that is life changing. For the students who failed to get level 2 at KS2; who have been in care; who are school refusers; who have been permanently excluded from other schools or who look after an alcoholic mother – the fact that you and your colleagues doggedly tracked their progress and intervened so that after a long tiring haul they got five A–C passes, however shabby, changes their lives forever. You make the difference!

Barber and Mourshed (2007) showed in three years between ages of 8 and 11 the difference in attainment between students with high-performing teachers and students with low-performing teachers was as wide as 53 percentile points. The quality of teaching in the classroom is the number one factor influencing student achievement. The quality of the school cannot exceed the quality of its teachers. Getting the right teachers in front of each class is a real challenge:

> *Within school variation in pupil performance is four times greater than between school variation. Much of this variation properly reflects the comprehensive student intake in the vast majority of schools. Yet government research in the UK suggests that there is still some 25 per cent of a young person's potential achievement that remains the responsibility of the school and its teachers.*

> Hargreaves (2003)

The difference between an effective teacher and an ineffective teacher is enormous. In one year the difference can be life changing. Ask any student who has endured a succession of replacement teachers, poor teachers, teachers who cannot communicate or who don't care enough to try and they will tell you. Teachers make a huge difference.

Work in the US by Sanders and others showed the difference over a period of a year made by the most effective as opposed to the least effective teacher.[33] Another researcher, Kati Haycock extrapolated these results over three years and made the point that the differences are so huge that it's the difference between a remedial class and a gifted and talented class.[34]

Teacher quality	Student achievement gain in one year
Most effective teachers	53%
Typical gain	34%
Least effective teachers	14%

When you factor in the quality of the school it can be seen that the differences are too marked to risk tolerating. Robert Marzano looked at the combination of teacher and school in 2000:[35]

Marzano's effects on student achievement of school and teacher effectiveness with students entering school at the 50th percentile	
School and teacher scenario	Student achievement gain after two years
Average school and average teacher	50th
Most effective school and most effective teacher	96th
Most effective school and average teacher	78th
Least effective school and most effective teacher	63rd
Most effective school and least effective teacher	37th
Least effective school and least effective teacher	3rd

John Hattie points out that, on the basis of 18 studies investigating the impact of teacher effects, somewhere between 7 and 21 per cent of achievement could be attributed to the teacher and that these effects were more marked in schools with a higher percentage of free school meals.[36]

Hundreds of thousands of teachers in thousands of schools do a great job. They do so and have done so in really challenging circumstances. It deserves recognition. A handful don't do a great job; they do an appalling job. They shouldn't be there and in most of these cases don't want to be there.

In the project schools, the school leadership teams did not tolerate mediocrity. One head teacher told me, 'I've got two satisfactory teachers but they're both leaving this year.' In another the head teacher had just found a post more suited to a member of staff in a nearby independent school and smoothed the path for her to leave. In another, a core of older staff had shown their preference for the previous management style by retiring early. An experienced head teacher in one of the 'outlier' schools said:

> There are only so many times they can turn it on in an inspection, but if they are not in it for the children it shows and I know I've done the right thing by intervening. Many other head teachers find the thought of confronting this hard but I don't. I just keep thinking it's the children's money! Every unwarranted absence, every day which is taken off for some spurious excuse, every early departure for a phantom appointment steals money from the children.

Don't turn a blind eye to or tolerate, mediocrity. Often people who under-perform are unhappy with themselves for doing so. They want help. Sometimes that's support, sometimes it's helping them leave.

The difficulties faced by schools that may have ineffective teachers were highlighted when a report published in November 2010 showed that in the preceding five years no teacher had been removed from post in nearly half of all education authorities in England.[37]

No one wants any teacher to lose their job but no student should have to suffer at the hands of someone who either isn't capable or isn't interested. One academic cited in the research claimed that 'identifying who is and who is not competent is hard because we cannot predict how much students learn by watching their teachers'. I wonder about the truth of this. It strikes me you can ask any student and they will tell you straight away; ask any other member of staff and they know who is up for it and who isn't; ask any leadership team and they will put the evidence in front of you. The issue isn't about identifying staff who are incompetent – that's easy. It's what can be done about it.

For middle leaders this is the most difficult part of what they do. There are two choices for staff who are not up to it: they leave or they stay. If they leave then there are two styles of departure – by agreement and with a blessing or through the competency procedures. If they stay then they either accept the need to improve or they don't. If they accept then it's knuckle down and agree a development plan. If they don't it's back to the procedures but this time it's kicking and screaming. No one wants this situation but to pretend it's not an issue or fail to acknowledge it causes huge disruption and demoralisation and exacerbates the problem.

In either of these scenarios it is vital to retain objectivity, separate the person from their behaviours and focus on facts. It's an emotional drain to argue over differences of opinion so focus on facts.

Recommendation for middle leaders: **monitor performance. The progress and results of any colleague or any student in your department should never be a surprise. Catch any potential problem early and intervene.**

Never walk by a misdemeanour. To do so is to sanction it and displace the responsibility for dealing with it to one of your colleagues. This is about setting and maintaining standards. Benchmark standards and model consistency. Standards can apply at different level: whole school, department, subject, team, individual member of staff or student. Whoever it applies to, strive for high and consistent standards.

One mechanism for benchmarking standards in teaching is to use a 'learning walk'. Our paper version of the learning walk takes the ten features of great learning:

1. Active engagement

2. Clarity of purpose

3. Use of assessment data

4. Organising and analysing information

5. Problem solving

6. Stretched through challenge

7. Demonstrating understanding

8. Progressing own learning

9. Reviewing and evaluating

10. Personalisation and enjoyment.

You could take your own and do what we have attempted to do by turning each feature into a continuum with keywords at each extreme. We provide these at the top of a landscape observation sheet with accompanying keywords, which can be selected using a highlighter pen. The keywords might look something like:

1. Active – Passive

2. Clear purpose – Without purpose

3. Informed by data – Uninformed by data

4. Analysing info – Accepting info

5. Problem solving – Answer collecting

6. Demanding – Undemanding

7. Show and share – Complete and confine

8. Independent – Dependent

9. Reflective – Unreflective

10. Personal – Impersonal.

Although the words themselves can appear pejorative on first reading what precedes their agreement is an extended discussion about the meaning that lies behind each word. This takes it out of being a highly personal judgement. Some schools prefer a grading or score against each word; others an interim word or phrase so there are three positions – active, occasionally active, passive. The essence of this is that it aligns with your broader agreed definitions of the features of great learning, it's quick, it's easily recorded and seen and, finally, it's developmental.

Recommendation for middle leaders: benchmark standards and model consistency. Standards can apply at different levels: whole school, department, subject, team, individual member of staff or student. Whoever it applies to, strive for high and consistent standards.

Internal variability should not be high. If so, try pairing the strong with the weak. Partner departments to share development meetings. Appointing a mentor who is a very good middle leader to the department might also help. Don't make excuses but have a vision and a clear idea about what you expect the department to achieve at the end of the year. Ensure that the targets are aspirational but realistic. Scaffold the challenge so that you are not aiming at 95 per cent A*– C if the department has never achieved over 54 per cent.

In *Heart of the Matter* published by NCSL (2003), there is this description of departmental meetings:

> *In our school, meetings run in threes. The first is an administration meeting, the second is a faculty learning meeting and the third is an inter-faculty learning meeting where we explore issues of teaching and learning. The last provides a supportive environment where middle leaders have opportunities to share good practice, coaching and mentoring.*

Try abandoning meetings that focus exclusively on administrative tasks. One middle leader described the benefits of doing so like this: 'No one liked them so when we agreed to change the agenda and have no mundane stuff it was like a weight had been lifted! Other departments started to do the same. It became much more professional, we planned them ahead and we got more out of them.'

Have an agreed plan to monitor student work on a regular basis. Cross 'moderate' and ensure that you do more than look at and mark books. Some contributions may be online or part of a blog or a wiki or some other electronic format. With books, write comments in the books to show parents you have seen the work. With electronic contributions, post or email comments.

In order to improve the depth and the range of monitoring, talk to an agreed sample of students. Do so for ten minutes and ask similar questions. Sit with colleagues in your department and agree the categories. Each interviewee must be someone they do not teach. Choose categories that will expose all participants to individual and groups of, students who might otherwise be labelled or treated as a stereotype. For example, identify five students who:

- say very little in lessons
- are high-ability but low-achieving boys
- are disaffected
- have interests which impinge on schoolwork
- have poor written work
- perform really well in some areas but not in others.

Focus discussion about data on individual students or very tightly defined groups of students. This takes you away from sweeping generalisations about whole classes or worse whole year groups.

Recommendation for middle leaders: **challenge mediocrity. Good enough rarely is. If you apologise for or overlook poor quality you allow standards to drop and all your colleagues suffer.**

19. Scanning:
stay ahead of the game

The head expects us to get out and see the best! She'll hear of something or meet someone at a conference or whatever and, before you know it, two of us are on our way! Personally I love that.

Middle Leader, St John the Baptist School

Scan the horizon. Keep your specialist knowledge up to date. Some subjects have a body of knowledge that shifts and expands. Exam requirements change, new syllabuses are offered and assessment gets altered. Stay abreast of changes. Summarise what's going on and share any developments with colleagues. The easiest way to keep up to date is by following exam boards and subject organisations on Twitter or via a RSS feed. Always send someone to the board meetings as they provide invaluable information and hints.

Share the costs with local schools to invite the examiner in to talk through trends.

Become an examiner and encourage members of your departments to become examiners. Try to get a GCSE and A level examiner in every department and certainly the larger departments. You get paid to have an understanding of the exam requirements, the ins and outs! This can be fed back. You don't have to do it every year! Exam results will improve!

Recommendation for middle leaders: **keep your specialist knowledge up to date. Some subjects have a body of knowledge that shifts and expands. Exam requirements change, new syllabuses are offered and assessment gets altered. Stay abreast of changes.**

Pioneer ideas and set an example. Any change requires energy to overcome inertia and circumspection. Say yes or no to initiatives and any change by gauging what's best for the students. Go out on a limb if you feel that it's worth it.

St Angela's School publishes a set of case studies each year. The publication began in 2007–2008 with four broad topics and twelve studies: raising achievement, pupil development and well-being, provision and staff development. They are excellent documents produced to a high standard. The impressive thing about them is they are all authored by different teachers who clearly have been encouraged to pursue an interest. The school gains but so do the teachers. Clearly the school sponsored these pioneering ideas convinced there will be benefits to students.

Most of the young teachers coming through have never known a world without the national curriculum! A system that teaches to the test, encourages the writing of schemes of work to a template and suggests covering every base in a written lesson plan breeds conformity over creativity. For some of your less experienced colleagues, particularly those who are younger, the fact that you support them in trialling an interest sends out a message that innovation linked to improvement is desirable.

Recommendation for middle leaders: where necessary, pioneer ideas and lead innovation. Make it easier for others to take risks in order to develop.

Don't waste time on a development strategy that misses the needs of your team or goes above their heads. If teaching in your department is barely satisfactory please don't spend time on 'How To Use Web 2.0 Tools' or 'Teaching Higher Order Thinking Skills' or 'Philosophy For Children'. All good stuff – but not yet! Get some basics in place first. Differentiate your support and do so based on genuine evaluation of needs. Similarly if you have subject specialists who are on their own, pair up with another school so they have someone to work with and if necessary pay for it. It's worth it as they can swap ideas and provide support.

Be reflective. Evaluate what you and your colleagues do. Ask what's gone well and what could be even better. Do so frequently and formally. Question what's become departmental tradition and precedent. For example, don't stick with a syllabus because you've always done it in the past. If you are thinking of changing, visit another school that does it. This will save hours and schools are really generous with resources.

Evaluation should not be synonymous with bits of paper. Don't burden staff with paper evaluation forms so you can collect them as evidence for a certificate, charter mark or standard. Any standard that ups the workload of staff and takes them off core purpose is not one that's worth having. Develop the use of simple review tools such as what went well (WWW) and even better if? (EBI) as a way of concluding meetings and of reviewing the week, half-term or term with staff.

Involve students in live evaluation as part of improving engagement. Have large posters around the school written by students all starting with, 'We like it when ...' 'We like it when teachers have a fun starter.' 'We like it when teachers set homework on the right evenings.' 'We like it when the teacher meets us with a smile.' 'We like it when the teacher knows our names.' Have them made professionally.

Recommendation for middle leaders: be reflective. Evaluate what you and your colleagues do. Ask what's gone well and what could be even better. Do so frequently and formally. Question what's become departmental tradition and precedent.

Scan the horizon to understand what's possible. Get out of school to see the best of what's around. If that's not physically possible, do so online. Collaborate like mad; share like it's only just been invented! Once you find a great organisation, website, network, school department or pioneer, then stay close. Save the best and abandon the rest! Drop what you find into the life of the department.

At Walthamstow School a group of about 25 staff meet once each half-term to discuss a book that they have read. The meetings take place either as a breakfast or lunch session. The books are chosen by the participants and are deliberately not too 'academic', too 'heavy' or too 'close' to the everyday challenges of the job. The book club disciplines discussion but it remains informal. Ideas are then followed up. Examples include books on contemporary trends, coaching and personal development and are chosen from popular authors.

Middle leaders should integrate professional learning and development with school and department priorities. Integrated development at St Angela's Ursuline School is the culmination of a long learning journey and a reflective culture across the school. It has some of the following features:

- Lots of lesson observations
- Classrooms with cameras
- Second year coaching scheme
- High quality publications produced annually to showcase the whole school learning interventions
- Meetings pared back to a minimum to allow improved CPD
- Thinking and learning centre
- Outstanding teacher courses
- Cognitive coaching.

The Harris Federation of nine academies in London has a common approach to issues like subject leadership in English, maths and science, continuing professional development and induction for newly qualified teachers. They have subject-based innovation groups led by a middle leader from one of the schools supported by a senior leader. Heads of department share data across the federation schools. They make observation visits to one another and share the design of innovative approaches to learning, lesson plans and the use of students as researchers.

The Wyre Forest consortium of seven schools is a voluntary arrangement that helps with shared post-16 provision. They identify common challenges for the schools across the consortium – for example, girls' underachievement in the sixth form – and then initiate research and training across all schools. On the last occasion I visited Haybridge two sixth-form girls from another consortium school were presenting their findings back to a large group of teaching staff.

Recommendation for middle leaders: scan the horizon to understand what's possible. Get out of school to see the best of what's around. Collaborate to advantage.

In ideal situations people make decisions rationally, concurrently and independently. In stressful situations people make decisions irrationally, sequentially and interdependently. The more influential the social network, the more we see this. This is why we get queues at petrol stations, runs on banks and huge sums of money spent on swine flu vaccinations! In a school, decisions are also influenced by a critical mass. In order to get tricky decisions through it's not force or quality of argument which will prevail, it's what the critical mass thinks.

In a process known as *social contagion,* how I behave influences how you behave and then in turn, how others connected to you behave. The best example is Stanley Milgram's popular pavement experiment from the 1960s. He planted actors or 'stimulus crowds' of different sizes to stare up at a window across a New York street. Passers-by were filmed to record their reactions:

- With a crowd of 1: 4 per cent of pedestrians stopped

- With a crowd of 15: 40 per cent stopped, 86 per cent glanced up

- With a crowd of 5 it induced almost the same effect as 15+!

What the people in your school think will be shaped by key influencers: people who have status; people who have knowledge; people who have strong friendship groups. Malcolm Gladwell in his book *The Tipping Point* called them *sellers, mavens* and *connectors.*

These people become most influential when interacting together. They become multiple persuaders! Work out who they are and when you have to initiate any change, work on them!

Once you identify sellers, mavens and connectors your persuasion strategies include:

- Selling *benefits*, not features – in other words explain the outcome which will benefit students and staff

- Attaching importance to behaviours which are *consistent* with values – ask what's important and what's believed: Is achievement for each and every student important? Do we believe we can make a difference for each and every student? Then let's do it!

- Using the *social cohesion* of the group – use multiple persuaders

- Giving something back in a *reciprocal* arrangement

- Exploiting *scarcity* of time, opportunity or cost

- Providing en*dorsements* from status figures – often the mavens.

Make informed and judicious decisions. Weigh things up. It's often better to sleep on it before replying hastily to that caustic email! Your colleagues will most often appreciate the steady over the spectacular. One school middle leader described to me how they 'tick, tick, tick along'. I don't see a contradiction between ticking along and pioneering change. I think it's about weighing decisions, avoiding premature rejection of possibilities, coming back to things and then once committed acting very decisively. In coasting schools innovation rarely gets to the point of discussion, often being dismissed as unnecessary for its own sake. In order to get things done use your influencing and persuasion strategies!

Recommendation for middle leaders: don't rush to judgement. Weigh things up. Once a decision is made, exhibit commitment and purpose in your support for that decision. In order to get things done use your influencing and persuasion strategies!

Appendices

The 10 x 10 project

The project was to visit the top performing schools in England in order to look for any patterns of similarity in leadership cultures and emergent school practices. The Specialist Schools and Academies Trust funded the project through Leading Edge. We originally started with ten schools and ten questions hence 10 x 10. We quickly expanded the list to get more balance and I renamed it High Performers!

Suggested structure for the school visit

- School visit – walk through with member of SLT (45 minutes)
- Interview with member of teaching staff who is relatively new to the profession and has at least two years experience of the school (45 minutes)
- Interview with two representative middle leaders (45 minutes)
- Interview with head teacher or principal (45 minutes).

Broad focus of each of the interviews

1. Core purpose
2. Student outcomes
3. Student learning
4. Classroom learning
5. Curriculum offer
6. Professional development
7. Staff roles, responsibilities and profile
8. The school as a community
9. Engagement with parents and carers
10. Engagement with the wider community.

SSAT criteria for selecting core schools

Outstanding Ofsted
At least three years of progress
Specialist 2008 and prior
CVA 2009 above expected
Low internal variability
JVA 5A–C 2009 equal to or above +10
JVA 5A–C EM 2009 equal to or above +10
2 A–C Sc 2009 above 54
2 A–C MFL 2009 above 32.

My criteria for selecting outliers

High CVA
At least three years of progress
Recognised nationally for an aspect of their work in leadership or in learning
Known to me
'Complemented' the core list by offering a novel dimension.

Limitations of the method

It's a snapshot
Visits were confined to a limited time frame
Schools chose the staff I spoke to
The criteria for schools selected promoted a particular view of success
I was the only interviewer.

Classroom teacher interview

Some typical questions which may emerge from the 'broad focus':

1. Core purpose

What do you see as the core purpose of the school? How are you supported in fulfilling the core purpose?

2. Student outcomes
    What do you wish your students to leave you and the school with?

3. Student learning
    How engaged are your students in their learning?

4. Classroom learning
    What does great learning look like in your classroom?

5. Curriculum offer
    How does what you teach match the needs and interests of your students?

6. Professional development
    How does the school support your professional development? Where do you see yourself in five years time? How will the school help you get there?

7. Staff roles, responsibilities and profile
    How do other staff help you professionally? To whom are you accountable? Who would you go to first if you felt you needed help?

8. The school as a community
    What does the school celebrate with most enthusiasm? Who gets involved? What are the key points in the school year?

9. Engagement with parents and carers
    To what extent are parents involved in supporting your teaching?

10. Engagement with the wider community
    How do you think the school is perceived in the wider community?

Middle leader interview

Some typical questions which may emerge from the 'broad focus':

1. Core purpose
    What do you see as the core purpose of the school? How is that core purpose communicated? How are you supported in fulfilling the core purpose? Describe the ways in which staff perceive and respond to 'core purpose'.

2. Student outcomes

What do you wish your students to leave you and the school with?

3. Student learning

   How engaged are your students in their learning? Is this consistent across the teaching in your department?

4. Classroom learning

   What does great learning look like in your classrooms? Do your colleagues share a view on what great learning looks like? Is learning actively discussed? If so how and where?

5. Curriculum offer

   How does what you teach match the needs and interests of your students?

6. Professional development

   How does the school support professional development? Where do you see yourselves in five years time? How will the school help you get there?

7. Staff roles, responsibilities and profile

   To whom are you accountable? Who would you go to first if you felt you needed help? In what way is performance data shared? How is performance data acted upon?

8. The school as a community

   What does the school celebrate with most enthusiasm? Who gets involved? What are the key points in the school year?

9. Engagement with parents and carers

   To what extent are parents involved in supporting the school?

10. Engagement with the wider community

    How do you think the school is perceived in the wider community?

Head teacher interview

Some typical questions which may emerge from the 'broad focus':

1. Core purpose

   What is the core purpose of the school? How is that core purpose communicated? How do staff perceive and respond to 'core purpose?'

2. Student outcomes

   What do you wish your students to leave you and the school with?

3. Student learning

   How engaged are your students in their learning? Is this consistent across the school?

4. Classroom learning

   What does great learning look like in your school? Do your colleagues share a view on what great learning looks like? Is learning actively discussed? If so how and where? How do you promote a focus on learning?

5. Curriculum offer

   How does what you offer match the needs and interests of your students? How is the curriculum offer formulated? How is it reviewed?

6. Professional development

   What is the school approach to professional development? How do you address any unevenness in the professional abilities and motivation of staff?

7. Staff roles, responsibilities and profile

   On what basis are staff appointed? Who is involved? How are expectations communicated to staff? How are staff supported in maintaining standards? In what way is performance data shared? How is performance data acted upon?

8. The school as a community

   What does the school celebrate with most enthusiasm? Who gets involved? What are the key points in the school year?

9. Engagement with parents and carers

   To what extent are parents involved in supporting the school?

10. Engagement with the wider community

    How do you think the school is perceived in the wider community?

The SSAT list

Sandringham School
Guru Nanak Sikh Voluntary Aided Secondary School
JFS School
Seven Kings High School
St Richard's Catholic College
Thornden School
The Thomas Hardye School

St Angela's Ursuline School
Comberton Village College
Northampton School for Boys
Haybridge High School and Sixth Form
Tudor Grange School
Walthamstow School for Girls
Dixons City Academy
Emmanuel College

The 'outliers'

Weydon School
Chafford Hundred Campus
St John the Baptist School
Alder Grange Community and Technology College
Paddington Academy

The journey to outstanding and beyond

Observable features of outstanding lessons

1. **Active engagement**

   - Choice

   - Decision making

   - Responsibility.

   'Students demonstrate excellent concentration and are rarely off task even in extended periods without direction from an adult.'

   They are involved in making choices and decisions over how they learn and assume responsibility for their own learning and the learning of others.

2. **Clarity of purpose**

   - Knowing what

   - Knowing how

   - Knowing why.

   'Students know and understand what they are learning, how they will be learning and why they are learning.'

   They know and understand the subject content, the process of how they will be learning and the benefits to them of the learning both inside and outside school.

3. **Use of assessment data**

   - Planning

   - Feedback

   - Differentiation.

'Students are given tasks that have been planned carefully to meet their learning needs based on assessment data.'

They have the opportunity whilst learning to get and give feedback. Tasks are adapted for individuals and groups based on this feedback.

4. **Organising and analysing information**

   - Identification
   - Investigation
   - Explanation.

'Students are able to find and analyse a range of information from a variety of sources.'

With the information they have found, they are able to identify patterns and trends as well as organise the results into a coherent explanation of the problem or issue being studied.

5. **Problem solving**

   - Focused on solutions
   - Strategies and tools
   - Questioning and creativity.

'Students are focused on the big picture and come up with solutions to problems rather than be focused on limited tasks.'

They are aware of, and persist with, a range of appropriate thinking strategies and tools to solve problems. They are encouraged to ask rich questions and be creative.

6. **Stretched through challenge**

   - Positive attitude
   - Resilience
   - Extending tasks.

'Students are prepared to tackle challenging tasks and issues with a positive attitude and are resilient.'

Learning tasks are predominantly 'low threshold, high ceiling' allowing all to be challenged.

7. **Demonstrating understanding**

- Variety of methods
- Application
- Grasp.

'Students are given the opportunity to demonstrate their understanding through a variety of methods.'

Their demonstrations show clear application to the problem being studied and real grasp of the core ideas.

8. **Progressing own learning**

- Commitment
- Self-assessment
- Improvement strategies.

'Students keenness and commitment to succeed and ability to grasp opportunities to extend and improve their own learning is exceptional'.

They are aware of where they are in terms of teacher and self-assessment and what strategies they can use to improve. Progress is at least good for some groups and is exemplary for others.

9. **Reviewing and evaluating**

- Focused on learning outcomes
- Ongoing in lesson
- Teacher-, peer- and self-assessment.

'Students have the opportunity, in a variety of ways, to review and evaluate against learning outcomes at appropriate times during the lesson.'

There is a culture of evaluation in the class where self- and peer-assessment is encouraged and improvement and progress is championed.

10. **Personalisation and enjoyment**

- Individualised
- Adapted
- Absorbed and enthused.

Learning is well adapted to, and shows an excellent understanding of, individual need. Students obviously enjoy their learning and show real enthusiasm in the lesson. They are absorbed with the learning tasks, want to know more and transfer what's learned beyond the classroom.

Learning review

Questions for staff interviews:

How do you know pupils are actively engaged in your lessons?

How do you ensure that pupils have clarity of purpose in your lessons?

How do you use assessment data in your lessons?

In what ways are pupils encouraged to organise and analyse information in your lessons?

How do you integrate opportunities for pupils to use problem solving into your lessons?

In what specific ways do you ensure that all pupils are challenged in your lessons?

What opportunities are there for pupils to demonstrate what they have learned in your lessons?

How do you integrate opportunities for pupils to extend and improve their own learning in lessons?

In what ways do students review and evaluate what they have learned in your lessons?

How do you know your lessons are personalised to the needs of your pupils?

Learning review

Questions for pupil interviews:

How much are you actively involved in doing things in lessons? Examples?

Are you clear about what you are learning in lessons and why you are learning about it? How?

Are you given feedback on your work in lessons? In what ways?

How much opportunity do you have to organise and make sense of information in lessons? Examples?

How much opportunity do you have to solve problems with others in lessons?

How often do you really feel challenged in lessons? Examples?

How much opportunity do you have to show what you have learned in lessons? Examples?

Are you always clear about how you can improve your work and learning in lessons? Examples?

How often are you given the opportunity to review what has been learned in the lesson? How is this done? When?

How much do you enjoy and feel enthusiastic about your lessons?

Observable features of beyond outstanding learning

1. **Proactive engagement**

   Students are involved in all phases of the experience, actively participating in choices over purpose, content, scope and methods of learning.

2. **Clarity of purpose**

   Students are clear about what, how and why they are learning and exhibit significant autonomy in how they will apply their learning.

3. **Ownership of the assessment process**

   Students develop and negotiate success criteria and the related assessment tasks and initiate self-, peer- and group-assessment.

4. **Organise, analyse and utilise relevant information**

   Students locate, organise and analyse information from a range of sources and then synthesise that information to progress learning tasks. In doing so they use thinking tools and new technology imaginatively.

5. **Direct enquiry and independent problem solving**

   Students define problems and work collaboratively and methodically to generate solutions at all phases of the learning process. They exhibit skills, practical problem solving strategies and use of relevant technologies.

6. **Stay actively involved at all stages of complex learning challenges**

   Students exhibit a 'growth mindset' showing self-awareness of themselves as learners, whilst remaining positive and engaged throughout.

7. **Demonstrate their own learning and understanding**

   Students elect to exhibit their learning and understanding using a variety of methods, opportunities and locations. In doing so they show depth of understanding and fluency in thinking.

8. **Measure and direct their own progress**

   Students are skilled at calibrating levels of progress and building self-evaluation into a repertoire of improvement techniques. They make decisions on how to progress.

9. **Habitually review and evaluate for improvement**

   Students seek opportunities, in a variety of ways, to review and evaluate against their outcomes at appropriate times during learning.

10. **Meaningful to the individual**

    Students show an enjoyment for learning and for autonomous enquiry. Learning is transferred and prolonged beyond the institution and so provides a sense of agency.

Leader recommendations

1. Talk up the positive aspects of your school experience. Do so relentlessly and unapologetically, and encourage others to do the same.

2. Use positive and inclusive words and images that have impact to communicate the best of your school.

3. Examine your school culture. Ask which cues a visitor might notice and, as a consequence, what conclusions they would reach.

4. Be clear on your core purpose. It's not a catch-all mission statement. It's a definition of what's fundamental to your operation.

5. Say no to initiatives and requests that do not serve your core purpose. Be ruthless in doing so.

6. Recognise that the journey to high performance may take five to seven years and plan accordingly.

7. Ensure the leadership team is visible and have a strong 'presence' around the school.

8. Obtain quick wins and initiate slow fixes.

9. Secure a framework for discipline and standards and strive for consistency of response to incidents from all staff.

10. Insist on lessons that engage, have pace, structure and challenge. An effective school is full of effective classrooms.

11. Ask hard questions about what's on offer in the curriculum and how it is accessed.

12. Build a sense of community through shared successes, symbolic moments and interventions.

13. Let staff know that if they do their best for students you will support them provided their best is good enough, and if not, you will act.

14. Get on top of the data, tighten monitoring and accountability and be open and honest to take staff with you.

15. Start to build productive partnerships but focus down to the 20 per cent that will give you the 80 per cent return.

16. Build a safe environment with strong school values where students and staff can focus on and enjoy learning.

17. Confront the challenge of creating autonomous learners who are skilled at learning and are also academically successful.

18. Generate and sustain whole school discussion about teaching and learning. Start by making it a standing agenda item on all school leadership and department meetings.

19. Review the quality of the learning experience against criteria that reflect the aspirations of the school. If you aspire to be world class in learning you have to go beyond the expectations of the inspectorate and the parent community.

20. Be aware of, and try to channel, healthy internal competition especially between larger departments.

21. Be prepared to be creative to recruit and retain great talent. Brilliant teachers can be like London buses. They don't often come by so take them when they come your way and find the posts or the contracts to do so.

22. Look at the criteria against which you recruit young teachers and learning support assistants. Is it too restrictive? Can you design a better alternative?

23. Put people before policies. Coercive, policy-driven leadership gets you compliance whilst supportive, policy-aware leadership gets you loyalty.

24. Create development opportunities by widening the school leadership team, breaking down larger responsibilities and creating new roles.

25. Protect the legacy whilst finding your own style.

26. Make every second school leadership team meeting a development meeting.

27. Focus down on what matters – planning, delivering, evaluating and improving quality learning experiences for your students.

28. Give as much attention to identifying and abandoning existing unhelpful practices as to searching for emerging innovation.

29. Identify the generic leader behaviours you wish to see modelled across the whole school community and, starting with the school leadership team, evaluate their impact.

30. Put a 360-degree feedback system in place for each member of the school leadership team and use this to develop a self-evaluation mindset.

31. Ensure you have a quality assurance system in place to ensure that for all stakeholders the school 'experience' is positive.

32. Put the most relevant student performance data into the hands of those who need it most, at the right time and in the most accessible format.

Teacher recommendations

1. Get the basics in place, build positive relationships and create high challenge low stress classrooms.

2. Be very aware of how your students frame success and failure. Encourage them to be incremental and focus on small performance improvements.

3. Sell the inherent value (benefits) to your students of engaging with learning.

4. Aspire to a broad definition of what the student experience will be when they are 'engaged'. Ask what engagement means from the learner's point of view.

5. Have high expectations – when you look at students do so in terms of their potential, not their past or their present performance – and prepare to be surprised.

6. Have a colleague observe your interactions with a range of classes noting who amongst the students gets your attention and what precipitates that attention.

7. Use their names.

8. Find opportunities for your students to see you in a different light. Take a responsibility outside of the classroom.

9. Position yourself as fallible: use a range of personas including the class dunce …

10. Develop the skills of mentoring, particularly the skills of building and maintaining rapport, asking good questions and listening.

11. Separate the person from the behaviours – use a range of imaginative strategies.

12. Use an agreed checklist of what constitutes great learning to help plan your lessons. Make sure all the elements are incorporated.

13. Define the classroom learning protocols you wish to promote. Display the protocols and reinforce them regularly.

14. Use Flip Video digital stills to debrief the three dimensions of learning.

15. Become more self-aware of what you do in the classroom and how it impacts on student learning: learn about your own teaching.

16. Widen your repertoire of classroom intervention roles and practise moving between them.

17. Recalibrate the orientation in your classroom away from performing and more towards learning.

18. Use a structure based on learning to design all your lessons and extended learning experiences such as enquiry and project-based learning.

19. Have learning conversations with your students. Build a vocabulary of learning. Focus discussion principally on the processes of learning, not on passing tests or question spotting for exams.

20. Use visuals to identify, reinforce and improve learning behaviours.

21. Provide opportunities for learners to demonstrate their independent learning skills. Such opportunities necessitate longer time frames, mixed groups, open-ended tasks with genuine outcomes.

22. Think strategically in preparing students for exams. Consider the social, emotional, physiological and cognitive dimensions to performance. It's not about cramming!

23. Use technology in service of learning and to attain your learning outcomes, not for its own sake or because it's inherently engaging.

24. Become acquainted with the basic classroom technologies and also have working familiarity with technologies that extend beyond the classroom.

25. Obtain a Twitter account and follow some of the leading educationalists and edu-technologists who post there. Attend TeachMeet events in your area.

26. Think beyond outstanding. Inspection criteria cannot be ignored but shouldn't become a brake on what's possible.

Middle leader recommendations

1. Write down your preferred role descriptor or words that best describe your role. Ask your 'team' to do the same for you. What terms are used?

2. Identify how you might find more opportunities to work with others to develop thinking on learning and teaching.

3. Look through the dimensions of the role. Ask yourself to what extent are you pursuing each?

4. Own the department and take pride in its contribution. Ensure your colleagues are clear on the wider benefits of the subjects taught and regularly share these with students as part of lessons.

5. Bring energy to what you do. Keep yourself physically, intellectually, emotionally and spiritually attuned to the rigours of the role.

6. Manage the budget. Take a responsible and realistic attitude to financial planning.

7. Plan short, medium and long term. Effort put into preparation and planning yields considerable dividends downstream.

8. Be resolute when necessary. The role is demanding and at times requires considerable determination. Being resolute should not however be confused with being dogmatic or parochial.

9. Understand learning. Stay up to date and professionally informed about new approaches to and understanding of learning. Encourage colleagues to do the same.

10. Identify components of both great learning and of great teaching. Ensure you and your colleagues understand that great teaching can only ever emerge from an understanding of learning.

11. Model high standards in your own teaching. Strive for constant improvement as a classroom practitioner and as a role model for others.

12. Know the students. Make it a professional obligation to know all the students. As students move into exam groups ensure that you and your colleagues have detailed profiles of past performance, future potential and unique qualities.

13. Observe others and give feedback on their teaching. Shift the culture. Go beyond performance management to create shared opportunities to plan, teach, observe each other and review for improvement.

14. Design or obtain a customisable, electronic observation system to avoid storing and transferring information from hundreds of sheets of paper.

15. Soften the hierarchy. Part of your job is to make it easier for others to do their job. Monitor and help manage the workload of your colleagues, especially those who are less experienced.

16. Interpret and protect the school vision. Be supportive of the school leadership team as far as is possible. Stay appraised of the facts, don't speculate about intentions or encourage others to do so.

17. Be positive and have consistent values. Focus on solutions; encourage others to do the same.

18. Establish and maintain orderly systems. Ensure that everyone is well informed about and understands the agreed working practices.

19. Communicate regularly and clearly. Publish the yearly cycle. Run all meetings with clear outcomes and action points. Use a departmental handbook as a reference and resource. Maintain it as a working document.

20. Be on top of performance data. Use data to drive department thinking about pupil performance and interventions. Ensure everyone understands the significance of data and can explain its relevance in simple terms to parents and pupils.

21. Motivate yourself and others. It's easier to stay motivated when there is strong buy-in to core purpose, when systems and structures are simple and helpful, when there is a team ethos and a sense of collective improvement. Motivation isn't about one-off speeches!

22. Involve others in decision making. It's not always possible to reach shared agreement, but it's always desirable to use a shared process.

23. Seek a balance of professional learning and development models to avoid over-reliance on one type of provision. Introduce a coaching approach.

24. Develop yourself, others and the team. Actively seek formal and informal opportunities inside and outside of school to enhance the professional capabilities of your staff. Where possible give responsibility as part of development.

25. Contribute to the life of the school. Departments can become isolated especially in larger schools. Encourage colleagues to take on whole school initiatives and opportunities.

26. Ask questions and encourage others to do so. Use departmental meetings and discussions as an opportunity to use some of the questioning and thinking techniques you would use in lessons.

27. Direct and be directive when necessary. There are some occasions when a direct intervention may be necessary. Sometimes this necessitates a fierce conversation.

28. Monitor performance. The progress and results of any colleague or any student in your department should never be a surprise. Catch any potential problem early and intervene.

29. Benchmark and model consistency and standards. Standards can apply at different levels: whole school, department, subject, team, individual member of staff or student. Whoever it applies to, strive for high and consistent standards.

30. Challenge mediocrity. Good enough rarely is – so if you apologise for or overlook, poor quality you allow standards to drop and everyone suffers.

31. Keep your specialist knowledge up to date. Some subjects have a body of knowledge that shifts and expands. Exam requirements change, new syllabuses are offered and assessment gets altered. Stay abreast of changes.

32. Where necessary, pioneer ideas and lead innovation. Make it easier for others to take risks in order to develop.

33. Be reflective. Evaluate what you and your colleagues do. Ask what's gone well and what could be even better. Do so frequently and formally. Question what's become departmental tradition and precedent.

34. Scan the horizon to understand what's possible. Get out of school to see the best of what's around. If that's not physically possible do so online.

35. Don't rush to judgement. Weigh things up. Once a decision is made, exhibit commitment and purpose in your support for that decision. In order to get things done use your influencing and persuasion strategies!

Endnotes

1. Hay Group (2004).

2. Deal and Peterson (2009), p. 11.

3. The Hay Group study did just this. The 2004 study explained some of theory of organisational culture and provided a really useful self-help exercise for a school community.

4. According to the McKinsey & Company Report (2010): 'A system can make significant gains from wherever it starts – and these gains can be achieved in six years or less.'

5. Seldon (2010).

6. See NCSL (2006), NCSL (2007a) and NCSL (2007b).

7. Pupils in advantaged areas are now six times more likely to go to university, while in the poorest constituencies, less than one in ten young people go on to higher education. In 2008, 23,000 students secured three A grades at A level, but only 189 of them were receiving free school meals, a core indicator of relative poverty. Quoted in Seldon (2010).

8. NCSL (2004).

9. Fullan (2010).

10. See Hanah Richardson, 'Top graduate teacher scheme "boosts results"', (accessed 16 February 2011). Available at http://www.bbc.co.uk/news/education-11743616 See also http://www.teachfirst.org.uk/TFHome/index.aspx.

11. *Daily Telegraph,* 30 November 2010.

12. See http://www.dcsf.gov.uk/pns/DisplayPN.cgi?pn_id=2010_0002 (accessed 16 February 2011).

13. Statistics cited in the unpublished report *Better Teachers, Better Teaching, Proposals from the 2010 Fellowship Commission*, National Leaders in Education. Seen by author.

14. Whelan (2009).

15. Barber and Mourshed (2007). Available at http://www.mckinsey.com/App_Media/Reports/SSO/Worlds_School_Systems_Final.pdf (accessed February 2011).

16. The classic 10,000 hours was first described by Ericcson (2002)and later picked up by Gladwell (2008).

17. Professor John Hattie, in a study of over 800 meta-analyses of what 'actually works' in schools to improve learning, found that heightened self-awareness of the processes which shape learning was one of the most significant factors: 'The biggest effects on student learning occur when teachers become learners of their own teaching and when students become their own teachers': (Hattie 2009).

18. Watkins (2010), p.9.

19. Glewwe and Kremer (2002).

20. Harlen and Deakin Crick (2002).

21. Nagy and Herman (1984), quoted in Marzano, Pickering and Pollock (2001), p. 124.

22. Watkins (2010), p9.

23. See Donald Clark Plan B at http://donaldclarkplanb.blogspot.com/search?q=wise.

24. Smith et al. (2005)

25. Cheng and Evans, (2009) survey, based on more than 11 million users, shows that 10 per cent of Twitter users account for 86 per cent of all activity.

26. Community Service was seen as a mechanism for delivering self-efficacy. See Sodha and Leighton (2009).

27. Author notes SSAT Keynote 2010.

28. http://en.wikipedia.org/wiki/Philippe_Petit

29. TASC (Thinking Actively in a Social Context), Thinking Hats and Kipling Questions (who, what, why, where, when, how) are tools to promote thinking.

30. See Smith, Jones and Kurlbaum 2010 pp.55-56.

31. Ibid.

32. Scott (2002).

33. Sanders and Horn (1994) and Wright, Horn and Sanders (1997), quoted in Marzano (2003), p. 72, from whom much of the material used in our arguments about effective teachers derives.

34. Haycock (1998), quoted Marzano (2003), p. 73.

35. Marzano (2000).

36. Hattie (2009), p. 109.

37. D. Sasson, We all want to see the back of bad teachers, *Times Educational Supplement*, 12 November 2010, pp. 30–31.

Bibliography

Ames, C. and Archer, J. (1988). 'Achievement goals in the classroom: Students' learning strategies and motivation processes', *Journal of Educational Psychology,* 80, 260–267.

Barber, M. and Mourshed, M. (2007). *How the World's Best-Performing School Systems Come Out On Top*, Washington, DC: McKinsey & Company.

Barth, R. S. (1991). *Improving Schools from Within*, San Francisco, CA: Jossey-Bass.

Black, P. and Wiliam, D. (1998). *Inside the Black Box: Raising Standards through Classroom Assessment*, Swindon: NFER-Nelson.

Bransford, J., Brown, A. and Cocking, R. (2000). *How People Learn: Brain, Mind, Experience and School*, Washington, DC: National Academy Press.

Brattesani, K., Middlestadt, S. E., and Marshal, H. H. (1981). *Using Student Perceptions of Teacher Behavior to Predict Student Outcomes*. Rockville, MD: National Institute of Mental Health; Washington, DC: National Institute of Education (ERIC Document Reproduction No. ED199297).

Buck, A. (2009) *What Makes a Great School? A Practical Formula For Success*, London: London Leadership Strategy.

Cheng, A. and Evans, M. (2009). *Inside Twitter: An In-Depth Look Inside the Twitter World*, Toronto: Sysomos Inc.

Collins, J. C. (2001). *Good to Great: Why Some Companies Make the Leap – and Others Don't*, New York: Harper Business.

Collins, J. C., and Porras, J.I. (1997). *Built to Last: Successful Habits of Visionary Companies*, New York: Harper Business.

Colvin, G. (2008). *Talent is Overrated*, London: Penguin.

Costa, A. L. and Kallick, B. (2000). *Habits of Mind: A Developmental Series*, Alexandria, VA: Association for Supervision and Curriculum Development.

Crossley, D. and Corbin, G. (2010). *Learn to Transform: Developing a 21st Century Approach to Sustainable School Transformation*, London: Continuum.

Davidson, H. (2002). *The Committed Enterprise: How to Make Vision and Values Work*, Oxford: Butterworth-Heinemann.

Deal, T. and Peterson, K. (2009). *Shaping School Culture*, San Francisco, CA: Jossey-Bass.

Dweck, C. (1999). *Self Theories: Their Role in Motivation, Personality and Development*, Philadelphia, PA: Psychology Press.

Dweck, C. (2006). *Mindset*, New York: Random House.

Ericsson, A. (2002). 'Attaining excellence through deliberate practice: insights from the study of expert performance', in M. Ferrari (ed.), *The Pursuit of Excellence through Education,* Mahwah, NJ: Lawrence Erlbaum.

Facer, K. and Pykett, J. (2007). *Developing and Accrediting Personal Skills and Competencies: Report and Ways Forward*, Bristol: Futurelab.

Fullan, M. (1982). *The Meaning of Educational Change*, New York: Teachers College Press.

Fullan, M. (1993). *Change Forces*, London: Falmer Press.

Fullan, M. (2010). *All Systems Go*, Thousand Oaks, CA: Corwin Press; Toronto: Ontario Principals' Council.

Galton, M. Hargreaves, L., Comber, C., Wall, D. and Pell, T. (1999). 'Changes in patterns of teacher interaction in primary classrooms: 1976–96', *British Education Research Journal*, 25(1): 23–35.

Gladwell, M. (2000). *The Tipping Point: How Little Things Can Make a Big Difference*, London: Little, Brown.

Gladwell, M. (2005). *Blink: The Power of Thinking without Thinking*, London: Allen Lane.

Gladwell, M. (2008). *Outliers: The Story of Success*, London: Allen Lane.

Glewwe, P. and Kremer, M., (2002). *Teacher Incentives*, Washington, DC: Brooker Institution.

Hargreaves, A. (2003) *Teaching in the Knowledge Society: Education in the Age of Insecurity*, London: New York: Teachers College Press.

Hargreaves, A. and Shirley, D. (2009). *The Fourth Way*, Thousand Oaks, CA: Corwin.

Harlen, W. and Deakin Crick, R. (2002). 'A systematic review of the impact of summative assessment and tests on students' motivation for learning', in *Research Evidence in Education Library*. London: EPPI-Centre, Social Science Research Unit, Institute of Education, University of London.

Harris, A. (2002). 'Effective leadership in schools facing challenging contexts', *School Leadership and Management*, 22(1): 15–26.

Harris, A., Andrew-Power, K. and Goodall. J. (2009). *Do Parents Know They Matter? Achievement through Parental Engagement*, London: Network Continuum Education.

Harris, A. and Chapman, C. (2002). *Effective Leadership in Schools Facing Challenging Circumstances*, Nottingham: National College for School Leadership.

Hattie, J. (2009). *Visible Learning: A Synthesis of over 800 Meta-Analyses Relating to Achievement*, London: Routledge.

Hay Group, (2004). *A Culture for Learning: An Investigation into the Values and Beliefs Associated with Effective Schools*. London: Hay Group.

Haycock, K. (1998). 'Good teaching matters ... a lot,' *Thinking K-16,* 3(2): 1–14.

Langer, E. (2009). *Counterclockwise: Mindful Health and the Power of Possibility*, New York: Ballantine Books.

Leadbetter, C. (2004). *Personalisation through Participation*, London: Demos.

Leithwood, K. and Jantzi, D. (1999). 'Transformational school leadership effects: A replication', *School Effectiveness and School Improvement*, 10(4): 451–457.

Leithwood, K. and Jantzi, D. (2006). 'Linking leadership to student learning: The contribution of leader efficacy', *Educational Administration Quarterly, 44(4): 496–528.*

Leithwood, K. and Riehl, C., (2005). 'What we know about successful school leadership', in W. Firestone and C. Riehl (eds), *A New Agenda: Directions for Research on Educational Leadership*, New York, Teachers College Press.

Marzano, R. (2000). *A New Era of School Reform: Going Where the Research Takes Us*, Aurora, CO: Mid-continent Research for Education and Learning.

Marzano, R. (2003). *What Works in Schools: Translating Research into Action*, Alexandria, VA: Association for Supervision and Curriculum Development.

Marzano, R., Pickering, D. and Pollock, E. (2001). *Classroom Instruction that Works: Research-Based Strategies for Increasing Student Achievement*, Alexandria, VA: Association for Supervision and Curriculum Development.

Marzano, R. J., Waters, T. and McNulty, B. A. (2005). *School Leadership that Works: From Research to Results*, Alexandria, VA: Association for Supervision and Curriculum Development.

Miller, W. R. and Rollnick, S. (2002). *Motivational Interviewing: Preparing People to Change*. New York: Guilford Press.

Mourshed, M., Chijoke, C. and Barber, M. (2010). *How the world's Most Improved School Systems Keep Getting Better*, Washington, DC: McKinsley and Company.

NCSL (2003). *Heart of the Matter: A Practical Guide to What Middle Leaders Can Do to Improve Learning in Secondary Schools*, Nottingham: National College for School Leadership.

NCSL (2004) *Learning-Centred Leadership*, Nottingham National College for School Leadership.

NCSL (2006). *Seven Strong Claims about Successful School Leadership*. Nottingham: National College for School Leadership.

NCSL (2007a). *What We Know about School Leadership*, Nottingham: National College for School Leadership.

NCSL (2007b). *Everyone a Leader: Identifying the Core Principles and Practices that Enable Everyone to be a Leader and Play their Part in Distributed Leadership*, Nottingham: National College for School Leadership.

Ofsted (2009). *Twelve Outstanding Secondary Schools: Excelling Against the Odds*, London: Ofsted.

Pollard, A. (ed.) (2010). *Professionalism and Pedagogy: A Contemporary Opportunity*, London: TLRP and GTCE.

Rosenthal, R. and Jacobson, L. (1968). *Pygmalion in the Classroom: Teacher Expectation and Pupils' Intellectual Development*, New York: Rinehart and Winston.

Scott, S. (2002). *Fierce Conversations: Achieving Success in Work and in Life, One Conversation at a Time*, London: Piatkus.

Seldon, A. (2010). *An End to Factory Schools: An Education Manifesto 2010-2020*, London: Centre for Policy Studies.

Smith, A. (2002). *The Brains Behind It: New Knowledge about the Brain and Learning*, London: Network Continuum.

Smith, A., Jones, J. and Reid, J. (2010). *Winning the H Factor: The Secrets of Happy Schools*, London: Continuum.

Smith, A., Lovatt, M., and Turner, J. (2009). *Learning to Learn in Practice: The L2 Approach*. Carmarthen: Crown House Publishing.

Smith, H. J., Higgins, S., Wall, K. and Miller, J. (2005). 'Interactive whiteboards: Boon or bandwagon? A critical review of the literature', *Journal of Computer Assisted Learning*, 21(2): pp.91–101.

Sodha, S. and Leighton, D. (2009). *Service Nation*, London: Demos.

Taylor, C. and Ryan, C. (2005). *Excellence in Education: The Making of Great Schools*, London: David Fulton.

Waters, T., Marzano, R. J. and McNulty, B. (2003). *Balanced Leadership: What 30 Years of Research Tells Us about the Effect of Leadership on Student Achievement*, Denver, CO: Mid-continent Research for Education and Learning.

Watkins, C. (2010). 'Learning, performance and improvement', *INSI RESEARCH MATTERS,* No. 34, Summer 2010.

Watkins, C., Carnell, E. and Lodge, C. (2007). *Effective Learning in Classrooms*, London: Paul Chapman.

Whelan, F. (2009). *Lessons Learned: How Good Policies Produce Better Schools*, London: Fenton Whelan.

About the author

Alistair Smith is an internationally known consultant, author and trainer. He has spoken to tens of thousands of teachers across the world and has written a number of books including: *The Brain's Behind It: New Knowledge about the Brain and Learning*, *Help Your Child to Succeed: The Essential Guide for Parents*, *Accelerated Learning: A User's Guide*, *Winning the H Factor: The Secrets of Happy Schools* and *Learning to Learn in Practice*.

Alistair is the chair of Alistair Smith Learning, a company committed to providing world class training and development programmes. He is the designated learning consultant to the Football Association, Patron of The Learning Futures Trust and an Honorary Teaching Fellow of St Mary's University College London.

Index